Immigration to the United States: Japanese Immigrants

Copyright © 2005 by Facts On File, Inc.

Facts On File, Inc.
132 West 31st Street
New York NY 10001

Library of Congress Cataloging-in-Publication Data

Ingram, Scott.
 Japanese immigrants / W. Scott Ingram.
   p. cm. – (Immigration to the United States)
 Includes bibliographical references and index.
 0-8160-5688-9 (alk. paper)
 1. Japanese Americans–History–Juvenile literature. 2. Immigrants–United States–
History–Juvenile literature. 3. Japanese Americans–Juvenile literature. I. Title. II. Series.
 E184.J3I54 2005
 304.8'73052–dc22

                                                                          2004014304

You can find Facts On File on the World Wide Web at http://www.factsonfile.com

Cover design by Cathy Rincon
A Creative Media Applications Production
Interior design: Fabia Wargin & Luís Leon
Editor: Laura Walsh
Copy editor: Laurie Lieb
Proofreader: Tania Bissell
Photo researcher: Jennifer Bright

Photo Credits:
p. 1 © The Japanese American Museum of San Jose; p. 4 © Bettmann/CORBIS; p. 11 © Bettmann/CORBIS; p. 15 © Michael Maslan Historic Photographs/CORBIS; p. 20 © Getty Images/Hulton Archive; p. 23 © Michael Maslan Historic Photographs/CORBIS; p. 24 © Getty Images/Hulton Archive; p. 27 © CORBIS; p. 28 © CORBIS; p. 31 © Bettmann/CORBIS; p. 32 © The Japanese American Museum of San Jose; p. 37 © Bettmann/CORBIS; p. 39 © Bettmann/CORBIS; p. 41 © Bettmann/CORBIS; p. 44 © Bettmann/CORBIS; p. 48 © U.S. National Archives and Records Administration; p. 51 © AP Photo; p. 54 © Getty Images/Hulton Archive; p. 56 © Getty Images/Hulton Archive; p. 59 © Bettmann/CORBIS; p. 62 © CORBIS; p. 65 © AP Photo; p. 67 © University of California Berkeley, Bancroft Library; p. 69 © AP Photo; p. 71 © AP Photo/Joe Marquette; p. 77 © AP Photo/Kenneth Lambert; p. 80 © AP Photo/Doug Mills; p. 86 © The Japanese American Museum of San Jose

Printed in the United States of America

VH PKG 10 9 8 7 6 5 4 3 2 1

This book is printed on acid-free paper.

Previous page: *A father and son pose in front of Dobashi market, a Japanese-American grocery store on Jackson Street, in the heart of San Jose, California's Japanese community.*

Contents

Preface to the Series

A Nation
of Immigrants

Robert Asher, Ph.D.

Human beings have always moved from one place to another. Sometimes they have sought territory with more food or better economic conditions. Sometimes they have moved to escape poverty or been forced to flee from invaders who have taken over their territory. When people leave one country or region to settle in another, their movement is called emigration. When people come into a new country or region to settle, it is called immigration. The new arrivals are called immigrants.

People move from their home country to settle in a new land for two underlying reasons. The first reason is that negative conditions in their native land push them to leave. These are called "push factors." People are pushed to emigrate from their native land or region by such things as poverty, religious persecution, or political oppression.

The second reason that people emigrate is that positive conditions in the new country pull them to the new land. These are called "pull factors." People immigrate to new countries seeking opportunities that do not exist in their native country. Push and pull factors often work together. People leave poor conditions in one country seeking better conditions in another.

Sometimes people are forced to flee their homeland because of extreme hardship, war, or oppression. These immigrants to new lands are called refugees. During times of war or famine, large groups of refugees may immigrate to new countries in

Left: Japanese immigrants responded to President Woodrow Wilson's 1917 call for Americans to grow their own food. This garden was farmed by 60 families near New York City. Each family farmed a 20-foot by 40-foot (6-m by 12-m) lot.

search of better conditions. Refugees have been on the move from the earliest recorded history. Even today, groups of refugees are forced to move from one country to another.

Pulled to America

For hundreds of years, people have been pulled to America seeking freedom and economic opportunity. America has always been a land of immigrants. The original settlers of America emigrated from Asia thousands of years ago. These first Americans were probably following animal herds in search of better hunting grounds. They migrated to America across a land bridge that connected the west coast of North America with Asia. As time passed, they spread throughout North and South America and established complex societies and cultures.

Beginning in the 1500s, a new group of immigrants came to America from Europe. The first European immigrants to America were volunteer sailors and soldiers who were promised rewards for their labor. Once settlements were established, small numbers of immigrants from Spain, Portugal, France, Holland, and England began to arrive. Some were rich, but most were poor. Most of these emigrants had to pay for the expensive ocean voyage from Europe to the Western Hemisphere by promising to work for four to seven years. They were called indentured servants. These emigrants were pushed out of Europe by religious persecution, high land prices, and poverty. They were pulled to America by reports of cheap, fertile land and by the promise of more religious freedom than they had in their homelands.

Many immigrants who arrived in America, however, did not come by choice. Convicts were forcibly transported from England to work in the American colonies. In addition, thousands of African men, women, and children were kidnapped in Africa and forced onto slave ships. They were transported to America and forced to work for European masters. While voluntary emigrants had some choice of which territory they would move to, involuntary immigrants had no choice at all. Slaves were forced to immigrate to America from the 1500s until about 1840. For voluntary immigrants, two things influenced where they settled once they arrived in the United States. First, immigrants usually settled where there were jobs. Second, they often settled in the same places as immigrants who had come before them, especially those who were relatives or who had come from the same village or town in their homeland. This is called chain migration. Immigrants felt more comfortable living among people whose language they understood and whom they might have known in the "old country."

Immigrants often came to America with particular skills that they had learned in their native countries. These included occupations such as carpentry, butchering, jewelry making, metal machining, and farming. Immigrants settled in places where they could find jobs using these skills.

In addition to skills, immigrant groups brought their languages, religions, and customs with them to the new land. Each of these many cultures has made unique contributions to American life. Each group has added to the multicultural society that is America today.

Waves of Immigration

Many immigrant groups came to America in waves. In the early 1800s, economic conditions in Europe were growing harsh. Famine in Ireland led to a massive push of emigration of Irish men and women to the United States. A similar number of

German farmers and urban workers migrated to America. They were attracted by high wages, a growing number of jobs, and low land prices. Starting in 1880, huge numbers of people in southern and eastern Europe, including Italians, Russians, Poles, and Greeks, were facing rising populations and poor economies. To escape these conditions, they chose to immigrate to the United States. In the first 10 years of the 20th century, immigration from Europe was in the millions each year, with a peak of 8 million immigrants in 1910. In the 1930s, thousands of Jewish immigrants fled religious persecution in Nazi Germany and came to America.

Becoming a Legal Immigrant

There were few limits on the number of immigrants that could come to America until 1924. That year, Congress limited immigration to the United States to only 100,000 per year. In 1965, the number of immigrants allowed into the United States each year was raised from 100,000 to 290,000. In 1986, Congress further relaxed immigration rules, especially for immigrants from Cuba and Haiti. The new law allowed 1.5 million legal immigrants to enter the United States in 1990. Since then, more than half a million people have legally immigrated to the United States each year.

Not everyone who wants to immigrate to the United States is allowed to do so. The number of people from other countries who may immigrate to America is determined by a federal law called the Immigration and Naturalization Act (INA). This law was first passed in 1952. It has been amended (changed) many times since then.

Following the terrorist attacks on the World Trade Center in New York City and the Pentagon in Washington, D.C., in 2001, Congress made significant changes in the INA. One important change was to make the agency that administers laws concerning immigrants and other people entering the United States part of the Department of Homeland Security (DHS). The DHS is responsible for protecting the United States from attacks by terrorists. The new immigration agency is called the Citizenship and Immigration Service (CIS). It replaced the previous agency, which was called the Immigration and Naturalization Service (INS).

When noncitizens enter the United States, they must obtain official permission from the government to stay in the country. This permission is called a visa. Visas are issued by the CIS for a specific time period. In order to remain in the country permanently, an immigrant must obtain a permanent resident visa, also called a green card. This document allows a person to live, work, and study in the United States for an unlimited amount of time.

To qualify for a green card, an immigrant must have a sponsor. In most cases, a sponsor is a member of the immigrant's family who is a U.S. citizen or holds a green card. The government sets an annual limit of 226,000 on the number of family members who may be sponsored for permanent residence. In addition, no more than 25,650 immigrants may come from any one country.

In addition to family members, there are two other main avenues to obtaining a green card. A person may be sponsored by a U.S. employer or may enter the Green Card Lottery. An employer may sponsor a person who has unique work qualifications. The Green Card Lottery randomly selects 50,000 winners each year to receive green cards. Applicants for the lottery may be from any country from which immigration is allowed by U.S. law.

However, a green card does not grant an immigrant U.S. citizenship. Many immigrants have chosen to become citizens of the United States. Legal immigrants who have lived in the United States for at least five years and who meet other requirements may apply to become naturalized citizens. Once these immigrants qualify for citizenship, they become full-fledged citizens and have all the rights, privileges, and obligations of other U.S. citizens.

Even with these newer laws, there are always more people who want to immigrate to the United States than are allowed by law. As a result, some people choose to come to the United States illegally. Illegal immigrants do not have permission from the U.S. government to enter the country. Since 1980, the number of illegal immigrants entering the United States, especially from Central and South America, has increased greatly. These illegal immigrants are pushed by poverty in their homelands and pulled by the hope of a better life in the United States. Illegal immigration cannot be exactly measured, but it is believed that between 1 million and 3 million illegal immigrants enter the United States each year.

This series, Immigration to the United States, describes the history of the immigrant groups that have come to the United States. Some came because of the pull of America and the hope of a better life. Others were pushed out of their homelands. Still others were forced to immigrate as slaves. Whatever the reasons for their arrival, each group has a unique story and has made a unique contribution to the American way of life. 🕸

Right: Japanese immigrants arrive in the port of San Francisco, California, in 1917. In this early wave, most Japanese were traveling from Hawaii, where they had settled in earlier years.

Introduction

Japanese Immigration

Seeking a Better Life

Among the many groups that immigrated to the United States in the late 19th and early 20th centuries, the Japanese have had a unique relationship with American society. While most immigrant groups come to the United States directly from their homeland, the first wave of Japanese immigrants came from what was then an American territory—Hawaii. When they arrived in the United States later, Japanese immigrants worked hard for a better life and made very important contributions to the United States. Despite these contributions, however, many Japanese immigrants often struggled against prejudice.

Across the Pacific

When the United States became a nation in 1776, Japan had been isolated from the rest of the world for more than 100 years. The isolation was partly the result of Japan's location off the Asian mainland. In addition, Japanese rulers prohibited foreigners from settling in the country. The people of Japan were also forbidden to leave the country.

Japan was ruled by an all-powerful emperor with support from a military leader known as a shogun. Enormous areas of land were owned by a few wealthy families who were loyal to the shogun. Their control of the land was enforced by warriors known as samurai who acted almost like a police force for the shogun and the wealthy families. Most Japanese people were poor peasants who worked the land owned by the wealthy families.

Japan's isolation ended in 1853 when American naval commander Matthew Perry sailed a fleet of eight American warships into Edo (today called Tokyo) Bay. Threatened by the strength and size of Perry's force, Japan's emperor signed a treaty, or agreement, that opened the nation's ports to the United States.

In 1868, a new emperor took the throne. He did away with the shogun and the samurai. This new ruler, known as the Emperor Meiji or "Enlightened One," was determined to force his nation into a modern era. He wanted to bring manufacturing, trade, and international relations to Japan. Thus, the last half of the 19th century was a time of enormous change in Japan.

Throughout the 1870s and 1880s, Japan's vast peasant class suffered because of those changes. In addition, many members of the old wealthy and samurai classes resented the change because they no longer had as much control. Violence broke out. This conflict and unrest caused many Japanese to want to emigrate to the United States in the late 19th century.

Japanese who decided to emigrate, however, generally did not go directly to the mainland of the United States. Instead, thousands of Japanese men went to the Hawaiian Islands between 1885 and 1894 to work.

In 1900, Hawaii became a territory of the United States. Although Hawaii was not a U.S. state, it was governed by U.S. laws, which meant that Japanese residents of Hawaii could more easily immigrate to United States. About half of the Japanese living in Hawaii did so, going to the West Coast of the United States. These first Japanese immigrants settled mainly in California and Washington State.

The Closed Door

In 1921, national quotas, or limits on the number of people who could immigrate from a certain nation or region, were introduced for all immigrant groups. While these laws severely restricted immigration from Europe, they excluded Asians entirely.

On December 7, 1941, the situation grew even worse for Japanese immigrants. On that day, a surprise attack by the Japanese navy on U.S. forces at Pearl Harbor, Hawaii, brought the United States into World War II, which had been raging in Europe for two years. Many Americans feared that Japanese forces would attack the country.

This fear caused widespread suspicion of Japanese Americans. In response to these concerns, the U.S. government had approximately 120,000 Japanese Americans living on the West Coast imprisoned in internment camps. More than 70,000 of them were American citizens. They had committed no "crime" other than simply being of Japanese descent.

Although strict anti-Asian immigration laws remained in place after World War II, more than 20,000 Japanese women who had married American soldiers and sailors stationed in Japan after the war came to the United States.

New immigration laws passed in 1965 opened the doors for many immigrant groups to come to the United States. But few Japanese wished to immigrate. Japan had recovered from the devastation of World War II, and its economy was expanding faster than the American economy.

In the late 1960s, young Japanese Americans born after World War II began to seek information about the Japanese internment camps of World War II. This interest led to the so-called redress movement, in which Japanese Americans sought apologies and repayment from the U.S. government.

Fewer Immigrants

As a result of decades of exclusion in the United States combined with the post–World War II economic growth of Japan, Japanese had little desire to immigrate to the United States in the second half of the 20th century. Japanese immigrants, once the largest Asian ethnic group, fell to third in the 1970 census. They were sixth among Asian groups in the 2000 census.

With fewer newcomers from Japan joining them, Japanese Americans in many ways became more American than Japanese. This shift, along with the change in societal attitudes toward minorities in the 1960s, led to a higher degree of acceptance for Japanese Americans. ◼

Opposite: *Shinto, a blend of ancient Japanese beliefs and elements of other Asian religions, was Japan's main religion from the early 1400s to 1945. In this picture, Shinto priests stand before a shrine to the powerful shogun Tokugawa Ieyasu in 1880.*

Chapter One

A Closed Society

Japan and the First Immigrants

People of Tradition

Today, there are more than 800,000 people of Japanese descent living in the United States. The largest numbers of Japanese Americans live in Hawaii and California. Like many immigrant groups of the early 20th century, Japanese Americans have largely been assimilated into American society. Most are third- and fourth-generation descendants of immigrants who left Japan in the late 19th and early 20th centuries. Many have married non-Japanese people.

Two traditions, however, have remained the same across the generations. One is a strong sense of family devotion to elders. The other is a deep belief in orderly and ethical conduct in society at large. These traditions come, in part, from the fact that Japan is an ancient island nation that was closed to the outside world for many centuries.

Japan

Early Japan

The beginnings of the nation of Japan are uncertain. There is, however, archaeological evidence that people lived in Japan around 10,000 B.C., when the four main islands that make up Japan were connected to the Asian mainland. In much the same way as Asian peoples migrated across a land bridge to North America to become Native Americans, prehistoric Asians also migrated to Japan. By the end of the last Ice Age, about 12,000 years ago, Japan had separated from the Asian mainland into four large islands—Hokkaido, Honshu, Shikoku, and Kyushu—and many smaller islands to the north and south.

> ## It's a Fact!
>
> In the Japanese language, Japan is known as Nippon Koku, the Land of the Rising Sun.

Japanese date the beginning of their nation's history from 660 B.C. At that time, on the main island of Honshu, the first emperor established a line of royal descent (the passing of the title of ruler to the oldest male child) from a mythical sun goddess. While the emperor ruled the country, much of the land was controlled by powerful nobles, or members of the wealthy upper class. Although the nobles were devoted to the emperor, they also built castles and had private armies to protect their lands from invasion by other landholders. Over many centuries, Japan was torn by minor battles and even civil wars between nobles.

For more than 1,000 years, Japan shared much of the tradition and culture of the Chinese civilization. The two languages were similar, and both civilizations had an emperor whose rule was supported by nobles and private armies. Buddhism, a religion that originated in India and flourished in China, was brought to Japan by monks in the sixth century. Buddhism taught that quiet, prayer-like meditation rather than the worship of saints or other religious figures was the path to happiness. The style of Buddhism that gained greatest popularity in Japan was the Zen branch of the faith. Zen beliefs emphasize that all people have the ability to achieve happiness, called enlightenment, through meditation.

Obon

One of the most important times of the year for both Japanese and Japanese Americans is the mid-August festival of Obon. Obon is a Buddhist tradition that honors the spirits of dead ancestors. It is believed that during these days the spirits of ancestors return to their former homes. To welcome them, Japanese light fires, pray, offer food at family altars, and hold dances called Bon Odori.

To prepare for Obon, people clean their houses and place vegetables and fruits as offerings to the spirits of ancestors in front of *butsudan*. These are Buddhist family altars, which are decorated with flowers and *chouchin* (paper lanterns) for the celebration. Obon begins when the *chouchin* are lit and Japanese go to family gravesites to call their ancestors' spirits back home. In some regions, fires called *okuribi* are lit at entrances of homes to attract the spirits.

Two nights later, the spirits are sent off again on paper lanterns, lit by candles placed inside, that are floated down a river to the ocean. Finally, on the next evening, the ancestors' spirits are guided back to their gravesites by the hanging of *chouchin* with the family name painted on them.

At about the same time, the Chinese philosophy known as Confucianism was also assimilated by the Japanese. Confucius, its founder, was a Chinese philosopher whose beliefs formed the foundation of Chinese society. He compared the relationship between a king and his subjects to that of a father and his children. In his view, children could live honest, good lives only if they obeyed their father no matter what. It was also important for parents to make decisions based on what was best for the family, rather than for personal glory.

Confucianism became part of Japanese tradition by being passed down through the generations as a belief that a person's only purpose was to help create better lives for others. No religious or inner-focused meditation was necessary to follow these teachings as it was in Buddhism. Becoming a better person meant serving one's family, village, or government.

Martial Arts

One of the most widely known of all Asian traditions in the United States today is the practice of martial arts. Perhaps the most popular of all the martial arts is the style of hand and foot fighting known by the Japanese word *karate.* This style of fighting developed on the island of Okinawa, which is located about 300 miles (480 km) south of Japan and due east of the Chinese mainland.

For centuries, Okinawa had been an important stop for Chinese trading ships, and the island absorbed a great deal of Chinese culture. This included the tradition of martial arts fighting called kung fu or wushu that had developed among Chinese Buddhist monks.

In 1609, Okinawa was conquered by the Japanese shogun, who promptly banned the possession of any weapons by the Okinawan people. In response, they began to develop a style of self-defense to protect themselves from the fierce samurai warriors. Adapted from China, it was called *te,* the Japanese word for "hand."

Over the course of several centuries of Japanese rule, the martial art known as karate or "empty hand" was developed. Karate, however, did not come to the United States with Japanese immigrants. Instead, the martial art was introduced to the United States after World War II by American soldiers who had studied it while stationed in Japan.

The arrival of Buddhism and Confucianism into Japan led to the development of Shinto, a religion unique to Japan. Shinto combines traditional Japanese beliefs, such as the worship of spirits that represent natural phenomena like the sky and the earth, with Confucianism and Buddhism. From Confucianism came the devotion to family and ancestors. From Buddhism came religious ceremonies and meditation.

In the 1600s, Japanese soldiers called samurai were enlisted to keep peace within Japan and carry out the wishes of the emperor. These samurai were photographed in 1880.

By 1600, Japan's nobles were forced to obey the rule of the most powerful military leader of the time, Tokugawa Ieyasu. The entire nation was ruled by Tokugawa, who worked for the emperor and was called the shogun. He did away with the private armies of the nobility and assembled a national military force to keep peace in the country and enforce whatever the emperor decided. The members of this military force were known as the samurai, and they acted much like national police. They were the only people in Japanese society who were allowed to carry weapons. Under Tokugawa's rule, foreigners were not allowed into Japan and Japanese were not allowed to leave the country.

The Opening of Japan

For more than 200 years, Japan remained an isolated country under the rule of the emperor, the shogun, and the samurai. Japan's economy was based almost entirely on farming, which in many ways was unfortunate for an island nation with a large population and a limited amount of land. Drought, crop failure, and starvation were common. More than 20 famines were recorded between 1675 and 1837. By the early 1800s, the poor peasants who made up most of Japan's population were protesting frequently against high taxes and food shortages.

Japan's isolation ended in 1853 when a fleet of eight American naval ships under the command of Admiral Matthew Perry arrived in Edo (Tokyo) Harbor. The American ships were steam-powered, paddle-wheel vessels, more modern than any ship in Japan. The American cannons on board were many times more powerful than the primitive weapons of the samurai. In a journal, Perry described the initial landing of the Americans to meet the Japanese representatives:

The whole number of Americans . . . amounted to nearly three hundred . . . very vigorous, able-bodied men, who contrasted strongly with the smaller and more effeminate-looking Japanese. These latter had mustered in great force . . . stated to be five thousand. . . . The loose order of this Japanese army did not betoken any very great degree of discipline. . . . Their uniform was . . . like ordinary Japanese dress. Their arms were swords, spears, and matchlocks [primitive guns].

During this first encounter, Perry was able to persuade Japan's shogun to sign an agreement called the Treaty of Peace and Amity (Friendship) that opened two ports to American ships seeking supplies. It also guaranteed that any American sailors shipwrecked near Japan would be treated well and returned to the United States. Another treaty was signed later that opened areas of Japan to American trade.

By the mid-1860s, five other European nations had signed trade agreements with Japan. The nation was suddenly thrust into modern economic relations that required a less rigid and traditional style of rule. Wealthy landowners, who wished to conserve their traditional hold over society, responded to the agreements with violence against both foreigners and other Japanese.

Eventually, however, these conservative landowners lost power and a new emperor took the throne in 1868. The Emperor Meiji–Japanese for "enlightened one"–soon realized that Japan was far behind the United States and European nations economically, socially, and militarily. Few national leaders have ever come to power more determined to force an entire nation to change. The desire to win the admiration and acceptance of Americans, in particular, became a driving force during the Meiji era.

It's a Fact!

The first Japanese immigrants to the United States brought mulberry trees, silk cocoons, tea plants, bamboo roots, and other agricultural products with them.

*The capital of Japan was moved to the port city of Tokyo in the late
1800s. In this picture, Tokyo is on the verge of expansion and prosperity.*

As part of the emperor's efforts to reform Japan, he
allowed Japanese to emigrate from the country for the first
time. As a result, in 1869, the first group of immigrants traveled from Japan to the United States. Under the leadership of
American John Schnell, Japanese immigrant farmers operated
the Wakamatsu Tea and Silk Farm Colony in El Dorado
County in northern California.

The U.S. Census of 1870 showed 55 Japanese in the United
States, all living in California. The farm's crops eventually failed,
however, and these first Japanese immigrants returned to their
homeland before 1880.

In the early 1870s, the emperor sent a team of Japanese
diplomats on a two-year tour of the United States. There they

studied the government, courts, prison systems, schools, factories, shipyards, glass plants, mines, and other businesses.
When they returned to Japan, the diplomats presented a long
list of ideas to reform Japan and help it catch up with the
West. Emperor Meiji believed that this new focus on a modern
Japan would make Japan the leading nation in Asia and
develop a strong sense of national pride among the people.

*Emperor Meiji, pictured with his family in the late 1800s, was
determined to modernize Japan and become an active participant in
world affairs.*

To make the country more accessible to foreigners, the
emperor moved the capital from the remote city of Kyoto to the
port city of Edo, which was renamed Tokyo. Japanese secondary
schools (similar to high schools), which were attended by the

children of Japan's wealthiest families, began to teach English. By 1876, Christian missionaries had established churches and schools in Japan to teach the religions practiced by most Americans at the time. Government textbooks encouraged young Japanese children to model their lives after Americans such as Benjamin Franklin and Abraham Lincoln.

As forward-looking as the emperor's plans seemed, in many ways they had a negative effect on the Japanese people. The move to a modern society required enormous amounts of money to pay for seaport improvements, factory equipment, schools, railroad and telegraph networks, and a well-armed military. Japanese peasants had always paid high rent to landlords for the lands they farmed, but now they also faced higher taxes, were forced into military service, and had to pay for education, which was now required.

Emigration to Hawaii

J apan under Meiji rule continued to be a nation in which average Japanese citizens had to struggle to survive. Now that they were allowed to leave the country, many Japanese workers decided to find new lives outside of Japan. They heard stories of workers in the United States earning five to ten times more than Japanese workers. Average Japanese citizens felt pushed out of their homeland by the difficult conditions, while at the same time they felt pulled toward the opportunities offered in the United States.

By the 1880s, large numbers of Japanese were eager to travel to the United States. Few, however, could afford the cost of the long ocean voyage. Therefore, when the opportunity to travel halfway there became available, thousands of Japanese took the chance. This was how the first wave of Japanese immigrants left their homeland for the island kingdom of Hawaii.

At that time, Hawaii was a monarchy, but most of the wealth of the country was controlled by Americans, who owned sugar, coffee, and pineapple plantations throughout Hawaii. These large farms required thousands of workers, but most native Hawaiians had died out due to disease brought by white settlers. This created a need for workers from foreign countries, and Japan became a leading supplier of workers for the plantations.

As part of its policy of opening itself to trade, Japan reached an agreement with Hawaii in 1884 that permitted contract workers to emigrate from Japan to the Hawaiian plantations. Under this arrangement, the plantation owners paid to transport the Japanese workers to Hawaii. There, the workers were required to work for a certain length of time, usually a year, and were paid very little for dawn-to-dusk labor seven days a week.

The opportunity to leave Japan, no matter what the conditions, was attractive to many young men. They had little chance of success in their homeland, and many hoped to save at least a small amount of money while they worked in Hawaii.

In 1885 alone, more than 30,000 Japanese men emigrated from Japan to Hawaii. Almost all became plantation workers in the sugarcane fields owned by Americans. The workers' lives were very hard. Many workers returned to Japan after only a brief time in Hawaii. Thousands of others remained, however, and Hawaii became the first stop in the immigrant journey from Japan to the United States.

Opposite: *A Japanese immigrant plantation worker carries a bundle of sugar cane on a Hawaiian plantation. In spite of the long hours, low wages, and backbreaking labor many Japanese people left Japan to immigrate to Hawaii.*

Chapter Two

From Hawaii to the Mainland

The First Japanese Americans

Plantation Workers

Despite the terrible working conditions, more and more young Japanese men emigrated to Hawaii in the late 1880s and early 1890s to work in the sugarcane and pineapple fields. Some were contract laborers. Others persuaded wealthier citizens in their home villages to pay the cost of their voyage to Hawaii, with a promise to repay the loan and an additional fee with wages they earned.

Under both arrangements, the population of Japanese immigrants grew enormously in the last decades of the 19th century. In 1890, the Hawaiian census listed 12,610 Japanese. By 1900, the Japanese population had grown to more than 60,000. Communities resembling Japanese villages, mostly populated by men, began to appear around the plantations. The arrangement between the sugar plantation owners and Japan provided an enormous benefit to the plantation owners while it brought thousands of Japanese to Hawaii. By 1890, Hawaii supplied more than 10 percent of all the raw sugar used in the United States.

Not surprisingly, the conditions under which the immigrants worked were very harsh. The fact that their supervisors in the fields spoke only English, which most of the workers did

A Japanese husband and wife work on a Hawaiian plantation near Honolulu in 1910.

not understand, made matters worse. Most Japanese felt as if they were little more than slaves. In 1893, one Japanese worker in Hawaii, Chinzen Kinjo, described a typical day: "Life on the Ewa Plantation was very hard; getting up at 4 A.M., breakfast at 5 A.M., starting to work at 6 A.M., and working all day under the blazing sun. We worked like horses, moving mechanically under the whipping hands of the luna [supervisors]. There was no such thing as human sentiment."

Hawaii Becomes a Territory

The lives of Japanese workers, however, changed a great deal in the 1890s due to political events. By the end of the decade, Hawaii had been made a territory of the United States. As a territory, Hawaii was governed by the laws of the United States. One of those laws prohibited contract labor arrangements. While workers under contract were required to complete their terms, they were free to find their own jobs once the contract period had ended. Because Hawaii was now a U.S. territory, the Japanese there were free to travel to the United States to seek work.

Throughout the political upheaval in Hawaii in the 1890s, Japanese workers continued to immigrate to the islands to work on the plantations. About 110,000 Japanese came to Hawaii between 1886 and the early 20th century under contract labor agreements. When the contracts expired, most workers either returned home or migrated to the U.S. mainland. About one-third, however, chose to stay in the islands.

By 1900, the mostly male Japanese communities that had been established around the sugar plantations included a growing number of Japanese women. Many left Japan to join fathers and brothers already in Hawaii. Others came to marry immigrants that they had never met. These marriages were often arranged ahead of time by family members in Japan. Such marriages were not uncommon in Japanese society at the time.

Hawaii

The history of Hawaii and the immigration of Japanese from that island nation to the United States were closely connected during the last decades of the 19th century. For most of the century, Hawaii had been a monarchy, with the crown passed down through a ruling family. By the mid-1880s, however, American business owners had made large investments in the Hawaiian sugar industry.

Most of the wealthy businessmen in the sugar industry felt that the monarchy had to be ended to serve their needs.

In 1887, a group of American and other white business leaders, supported by a private armed force, imposed a new constitution on the Hawaiian king, Kamehameha, that made him little more than a figurehead. This constitution, called the Bayonet Constitution, also excluded three-fourths of native Hawaiians, who were mostly poor, as well as Asian immigrants, from voting.

This new constitution infuriated many Hawaiians. King Kamehameha was succeeded by Queen Liliuokalani, who rejected the Bayonet Constitution. In January 1893, the queen attempted to replace the Bayonet Constitution with a constitution that was fairer to native Hawaiians. In response, powerful white leaders took over government buildings in the capital city, Honolulu, and overthrew the queen. Claiming that Hawaii was now a free nation, the rebels placed wealthy planter Sanford B. Dole, the son of an American missionary, in the position of president.

For the next several years, the "free" republic of Hawaii attempted to become part of the United States. Meanwhile, the large deepwater port at Pearl Harbor became a key U.S. naval base for warships crossing the Pacific. Finally, in June 1900, Hawaii became a U.S. territory. Dole was appointed the first territorial governor.

*Queen Liliuokalani attempted to draft a constitution that reestablished
the civil rights of native Hawaiians.*

Japanese men in Hawaii outnumbered women by more
than seven to one in 1886, but the arrival of more and more
Japanese women steadily decreased this ratio to slightly more
than two to one in the early 1900s. As the Japanese married and
had children, their communities in Hawaii grew. Japanese immigrants gradually built a permanent presence in the Hawaiian
Islands. By 1910, Japanese immigrants made up nearly 40
percent of the islands' population.

After Hawaii became a U.S. territory and contract labor
became illegal, Japanese workers, who made up most of Hawaii's

workforce, felt that they had the right to protest the terrible working conditions. In 1908, Japanese workers went on strike to demand better wages and working conditions at sugar plantations in Hawaii. The strike failed to achieve these goals, partly because the Japanese did not have the support of immigrant workers from other ethnic groups. Nevertheless, the protest served as an early example of a united immigrant community action.

After the unsuccessful strike, Japanese workers grew more and more dissatisfied with the conditions on Hawaiian planta- tions. As a result, more than 40,000 Japanese left Hawaii to find jobs in the United States in the years immediately after 1908. While there were already several thousand Japanese in the United States (they had emigrated as soon as Hawaii became a territory), this mass movement from Hawaii became the first large wave of Japanese immigration to the United States.

Working hard paid off for many Japanese immigrants, who became landowners themselves in time. The Kawahara family, pictured here in the late 1920s, ran one of the successful Japanese farming operations in California.

Kagamiwari

One of the most popular customs in Japan and in Japanese-American communities is the breaking open of the sake barrel, an event known as *kagamiwari*. Sake, a wine made from rice, is a traditional beverage in Japan. The act of breaking open the top of a wooden barrel containing sake is considered good luck.

Kagamiwari is part of holidays such as New Year's Day, the most popular holiday in Japan. It is also part of wedding ceremonies, as a way to wish newlyweds good fortune. *Kagamiwari* is also frequently done when a new company is opened or a ship is launched.

Early Immigrants in the United States

Those in this first large wave of Japanese immigrants to the United States found it relatively easy to get work. Ironically, there was a shortage of workers for low-skilled jobs because of anti-immigrant laws against Chinese. Immigration from China to the United States had been prohibited since 1882. Chinese who had come to the United States before that time had taken many of the lowest-wage jobs available. As these workers grew older, a need arose for new immigrant workers. A large number of jobs became available in railroad construction, logging, mining, fishing, and meatpacking.

Although many of the Japanese immigrants found work in city factories and in construction, many others chose to work on farms. Most had grown up as farmers in Japan or Hawaii, and western states, especially California, offered great farming opportunities. Since many of these immigrants had come from a tradition of working on land owned by others, the possibility of owning and farming land of their own was extremely attractive. The fertile valleys of California offered an almost limitless supply of land and work to eager immigrants.

Japanese workers soon acquired a reputation as hard workers who accepted low pay, long hours, and difficult conditions without complaint. As field workers who were paid by the amount of produce they picked, Japanese generally earned twice as much as other workers because they were so good at their jobs.

Many Japanese farmworkers soon became landowners themselves. Like other immigrant laborers of the time, Japanese farmworkers often went from field to field to work in groups, under a fellow Japanese supervisor who spoke English. As they traveled around the farmlands of California, Japanese workers pooled their money to buy farmland. Japanese immigrants were one of the most successful immigrant groups to combine their individual resources for the benefit of all. Using these resources allowed Japanese immigrants to establish farms on more than 50,000 acres (20,000 ha) in California by 1904. By 1909, that figure had grown to more than 150,000 acres (60,000 ha).

Japanese farmers were extremely efficient and resourceful. Using traditional farming techniques that had been successful in Japan over the course of many centuries, they often were able to coax more crops out of less land than white farmers. Often, the land the Japanese farmed in California was sandy and less fertile than that farmed by whites. Yet the Japanese farmers overcame such obstacles. In the semidesert area of Florin, California, for

It's a Fact!

By 1919, Japanese farms in California earned more than $67 million. In today's money, that is nearly $700 million.

example, Japanese Americans found sandy soil ideal for growing grapes and strawberries. They planted strawberries between rows of grapevines. They could then sell the quick-growing strawberries during the five years it would take the grapevines to yield fruit. Within the first decades of the 20th century, Japanese farmers became the leading producers of strawberries and grapes. Florin eventually became known as the strawberry capital of California.

The Potato King

George Shima of California was one of the most successful Japanese immigrants to the United States during this time. Shima, whose real name was Kinji Usima, was born in Japan in 1863. He came to the United States in 1889 with only a few dollars in his pocket. Shima was able to find work in the farmlands of northern California, where the need for field workers and the anti-Chinese laws of the time provided his opportunity.

By working long hours and saving money, Shima was able to buy land of his own to farm. In the early 1900s, he became the first person to plant potatoes in California, farming several hundred acres outside of the state capital at Sacramento. By 1910, Shima controlled more than 20,000 acres of land and was known as California's "Potato King." His large-scale operation, called "factories in the field," made Shima one of California's wealthiest men by the time he died in 1926.

Other Japanese farmers had similar success across California. In Walnut Grove, farmers produced hops for brewing and vegetables such as asparagus. Marysville and Loomis farmers produced vegetables and pears. In Colusa, Japanese rice farmers were so successful that several rice companies developed under the ownership of Japanese-American farmers.

Anti-Japanese Discrimination

T he qualities that made the Japanese one of the most successful immigrant groups to come to the United States, however, quickly turned other Americans against them. Because Japanese made excellent employees, they were envied—and then hated—by American workers, who felt that the Japanese immigrants were taking jobs away from other Americans. Labor unions (organizations that fought for the rights of workers) also resented Japanese workers because they were widely admired by bosses. Labor union officials assumed that Japanese workers would side with the bosses

Discrimination against Japanese immigrants grew as the Japanese community prospered. Signs such as these posted on a home in Hollywood, California, in 1923 were common in some communities.

in any struggle the unions had with employers for workers' rights. Samuel Gompers, the leader of the American Federation of Labor (AFL), the first national labor union in the United States, refused to let Japanese workers join his organization.

Japanese immigrants soon faced similar discrimination from the American business and farming communities. While American factory owners and farmers had welcomed the Japanese as low-paid workers, they feared them as successful farmers and business rivals. This business rivalry was often based on the kind of racial prejudice that many Americans felt against Japanese and other Asian immigrants.

These racist attitudes found support at all levels of American society and government. Organizations that worked to stop immigration to the United States had turned their focus on Japanese by 1905 even as the first wave of Japanese immigrants was arriving from Hawaii. That year, the Asiatic Exclusion League (AEL) was formed in California. The goal of the AEL was to prevent Japanese immigrants from coming to the United States.

> # It's a Fact!
>
> When Japanese students in San Francisco public schools were ordered to attend the Oriental School in 1906, there were just 93 of them. Twenty-five of the students had been born in the United States and were American citizens.

The group also tried to segregate Japanese already in the United States, which meant that it wanted to keep Japanese people separate from other Americans. Under pressure from the AEL, for example, the San Francisco Board of Education ruled in 1906 that all Japanese students should join the Chinese at the segregated Oriental School, which had been established in 1884.

The most extreme anti-Japanese measure occurred as a result of the actions of the U.S. government. In 1907, President Theodore Roosevelt was under intense pressure from anti-immigrant groups to stop immigration from Japan. They urged Roosevelt to support a law similar to the Chinese Exclusion Act, which had been passed in 1882. This law simply shut the door on all immigrants from China. The anti-immigrant groups hoped to stop Japanese immigration in the same way.

By 1907, however, Japan had become not only modernized, but the strongest military power in Asia. Roosevelt did not want to anger Japanese leaders. He also disliked the racist attitudes of groups such as the AEL. He called their actions "foolish offensiveness" and their leaders "idiots." When anti-Japanese riots broke out in San Francisco, Roosevelt worried that the "mob of a single city may perform acts of lawless violence that would plunge us into war" with Japan.

Nevertheless, the pressure to take steps against Japanese immigration remained intense. Roosevelt vetoed (voted against) several bills that were aimed at stopping Japanese immigration, preventing them from becoming laws. In 1907, however, Roosevelt finally reached the so-called Gentlemen's Agreement with Japan. Under this agreement, the Japanese government agreed to prohibit male laborers from emigrating to Hawaii or the U.S. mainland. In return, the United States agreed to allow Japan to send "the parents, wives, and children of laborers" who already lived in the United States.

This agreement between Japan and the United States caused a change in the pattern of Japanese immigration almost overnight. The first wave of immigration ended abruptly, but the next wave led to the establishment of a permanent Japanese-American community in the United States. 🀫

Opposite: The wives and children of Japanese laborers were permitted entry to the United States in 1907 by the Gentlemen's Agreement with Japan. In this picture, Japanese children at Angel Island await entry into the port of San Francisco to meet their father.

Chapter Three

The Door Closes

Anti-Immigration Laws

Picture Brides

The Gentlemen's Agreement of 1907 between the United States and Japan had two immediate effects. First, it reduced the number of Japanese immigrants coming to the United States by more than 30 percent. More important, however, for the growth of the Japanese-American population, the immigrants who came after 1907 were overwhelmingly female. In 1900, the U.S. Census counted 24,326 Japanese in the United States. Of that number, just 410 were female. In other words, there were about 20 times more Japanese-American men than women at that time. By 1910, there were only about seven times more Japanese men than women in the United States. By 1920, the ratio of Japanese men to women was two to one. This was similar to the population changes that had occurred in Hawaii as Japanese communities formed there.

It's a Fact!

Between 1910 and 1920, an estimated 19,000 picture brides went through Angel Island.

Some of the Japanese women who came to the United States after 1907 were wives joining their husbands. Many others, however, were what came to be known as "picture brides," who were coming to marry men they had never seen. Such arranged marriages were common at the time in Japan and in other cultures. In a traditional arranged marriage, a man and woman were matched by their families on the basis of social status, personality, and background. Many arranged marriages had taken place among the Japanese immigrants in Hawaii.

By the early 1900s, photography was common enough that brides and grooms in arranged marriages could exchange photographs between Japan and the United States. Once an arrangement was made, a Japanese-American man who could afford to travel to Japan returned there to be married and would then return to the United States with his immigrant bride.

Many picture brides, however, traveled to the United States alone because their grooms could not afford the trip to Japan. Those who entered the United States after 1910 were immediately sent to Angel Island, an immigration facility in San Francisco Bay. At Angel Island, all immigrants from Asia were processed, meaning that their travel documents were examined, their names were entered in a census register, and they were given medical exams. It was at Angel Island that most picture brides saw their new husbands for the first time.

Congressional representative John Raker (holding documents) examined the passports of these Japanese picture brides shortly after they arrived at the Angel Island Immigration Station in 1920. Raker led an effort to restrict immigration from Japan and other Asian countries.

Angel Island

Beginning in 1910, all immigrants to the West Coast of the
United States, both male and female, were required to enter
the country at San Francisco, California. There the newcomers
passed through Angel Island. The station at Angel Island had been
built to process immigrants as they entered the United States. But
because most of the immigrants who landed there were Asian, in
reality the main objective at Angel Island was to find any way
possible to exclude the new arrivals and send them back home.

This process began as soon as a boatload of immigrants
arrived in San Francisco. All passengers would be separated by
nationality. Europeans or travelers with first- or second-class
tickets would be processed on the ship and allowed to disembark
and enter the country. Asians and other immigrants, including
Russians and Mexicans, however, would be ferried to Angel
Island, the largest island in San Francisco Bay.

At the immigration station, men were separated from women
and children, and all were given complete medical exams. This
was a deeply embarrassing experience for Japanese and other
Asians, because Asian medical practice did not include disrobing
in front of strangers or being poked with metal instruments. After
examination, the immigrants were then assigned to a bunk in a
detention dormitory, which was little more than a prison building.
There they awaited interrogation (questioning) by the Board of
Special Inquiry.

For the interrogation, an immigrant was called before a
board of two immigrant inspectors, a recording secretary, and a
translator, who helped the Japanese-speaking immigrants and the
English-speaking American officials understand one another.
Interrogations could last many hours and even days. During this
time, immigrants lived like prisoners. Living conditions were

terrible, and the food was barely edible. In 1910, Luther Steward, acting commissioner for the Immigration Service in San Francisco, wrote of the barracks, "If a private individual had such an establishment, he would be arrested by local health authorities."

Anti-Japanese Laws

D espite the reduction in the number of Japanese workers coming to the United States due to the Gentlemen's Agreement, anti-Japanese prejudice continued to increase up and down the Pacific coast where the immigrants had settled. This prejudice was an example of nativism, a negative attitude toward immigrants in general, which spread across the United States during the early 20th century. The prejudice was especially negative toward immigrants from areas other than northern Europe.

One of the most powerful nativist groups was the Immigration Restriction League (IRL), which had been founded by several wealthy easterners at the turn of the century to fight the wave of immigrants whom they considered "different" or "foreigners." The founder of the group, Prescott Hall, said that it was up to Americans to decide what groups should populate the United States. He suggested that British, German, and other northern European people were the best choice, since they were "historically free, energetic, [and] progressive." In contrast, Hall claimed that Jews and other people from eastern and southern Europe, as well as Asians, were "historically downtrodden," primitive, and lazy. Many people in the late 19th and early 20th centuries shared Hall's racism.

The IRL, like other anti-immigration groups, pressured the U.S. government to pass laws aimed at halting immigration. One such law, for example, would require all immigrants to be able to read English in order to be admitted to the United States. Since most immigrants were unable to do this, such a law would cut down on the number of immigrants who could enter the country.

While the IRL was the most active group working to stop immigration in general throughout the United States, the Asian Exclusion League (AEL) was the most powerful group on the West Coast. For most of the first two decades of the 20th century, the AEL encouraged discrimination against Japanese immigrants. It claimed that Japanese immigrants working in the United States sent the money they earned back to Japan, unlike white workers, who kept their money in the United States, where it could benefit the American economy.

Anti-immigrant groups were common in the first few decades of the 20th century. This sign posted by an organization called the Anti-Alien Association appeared in Phoenix, Arizona, in 1935.

The AEL also accused the immigrants of taking jobs from whites by working for less money in worse conditions. In fact, the hardworking Japanese quickly left behind their original low-wage jobs. Farming, in particular, provided a path to rapid success. After starting as ordinary laborers, many Japanese progressed to leasing land for farming and then to purchasing land for their own small farms.

Yet even this pursuit of what most people might call the "American Dream" met with objections from the AEL and others. Under pressure from the AEL, Oregon passed a law in 1907 stating that Japanese could never become permanent residents of the state. A newspaper editorial warned, "on the far out-posts of the Western world rises the specter of the yellow [referring to the skin tone of Asian peoples] peril. . . . It is nothing more or less than a threatening inundation [flood] . . . over the Pacific Ocean."

Nowhere was the anti-immigrant feeling more intense than in California. From 1909 on, anti-Japanese bills were introduced in the California legislature every year until after World War II (1939–1945). The first anti-Japanese law to take effect in California was the Webb-Hartley Law, commonly known as the Alien Land Law of 1913. This law said that "aliens [foreigners] ineligible to citizenship" could lease land for only three years. It also barred those same aliens from purchasing any land in the future. Changes to the law in 1919 and 1920 further restricted land-leasing agreements for all Asian Americans.

Although the law did not mention ethnic groups by name, it was clear that "aliens ineligible to citizenship" included the Japanese, who were banned by law in some states from becoming U.S. citizens. In 1922, Japanese immigrant Takao Ozawa fought this ban all the way to the U.S. Supreme Court. In the case of *Takao Ozawa v. the United States,* the Court declared that, according to the U.S. Constitution, citizenship was limited only to "free white persons" and "those of African descent." Thus, no matter how long an issei, or first-generation Japanese immigrant, had been in the United States, he or she could never be a U.S. citizen. Children born to issei in the United States, known as nisei, however, were considered citizens.

Other laws passed by the California state government were aimed at weakening small businesses owned by immigrants, including the Japanese. Among the legislation were laws that banned Asian business owners, primarily Japanese, but some from India, from hiring white women and from inheriting land. In an effort to weaken the success of Japanese commercial fishermen in southern California, the cost of a fishing license was increased for any person of Asian descent.

California state officials readily admitted the aim of these laws. In 1914, one official said, "The fundamental basis of all legislation has been, and is, race undesirability. It seeks to limit the Japanese presence by curtailing [limiting] the privileges they enjoy here. And it seeks to limit the numbers who will come by limiting the opportunities for [them] when they arrive."

It's a Fact!

The financial assistance groups formed by Japanese immigrants in the early 1900s were called *tanomoshi*, a Japanese word that means "to ask for help."

Despite the widespread support for the anti-Japanese efforts, Japanese immigrants continued to succeed. They pooled their resources to form financial assistance groups. These organizations offered financial services such as loans, savings accounts, and investment opportunities that regular banks refused to Japanese. Such organizations led to a greater sense of community among Japanese immigrants, who, despite the intense discrimination they faced, had begun to see themselves as Japanese Americans.

Terminal Island

In the early 1900s, an issei immigrant named Hamashita settled on Terminal Island, also called San Pedro Island, off the coast of Los Angeles. At first, Hamashita would row his small boat to the areas offshore where schools of tuna were known to feed, catching them with a fishing rod. Eventually he began to use a motorboat and fishing nets, which allowed him to catch far more fish than a rod. Hamashita then brought his catch ashore for drying and canning.

By 1907, several hundred Japanese fishermen had moved to Terminal Island. Small canning companies were started on the island, creating a market for the fishing fleet's catch. The canned fish was then transported to stores to be sold. The establishment of canneries created many jobs for Japanese immigrants and their families. To attract these families, cannery owners built small houses that soon became home to fishermen, cannery workers, and their families. In 1916, Fishermen Hall, a community center, was built on Terminal Island.

By 1929, it is estimated that there were 900 Japanese fishermen on Terminal Island catching fish for the canneries. Tuna Street was the center of the Japanese community, with restaurants, grocery stores, pool halls, barbershops, and a meat market owned by Japanese issei and later by nisei.

In 1942, more than 3,000 Japanese Americans lived on Terminal Island. That year, it became the first community to be forcibly evacuated to internment camps by the U.S. government. When the Japanese left, the fishing industry vanished from Terminal Island, too. Today, nothing remains of the Japanese community that was the foundation of California's huge fishing industry.

The Nisei Generation

The laws aimed at limiting the opportunities of Japanese Americans were only partly successful. Anti-immigrant laws did not apply to Japanese-American children born in the United

States. These children were American citizens and therefore permitted to own land. Japanese immigrant parents frequently purchased land under the names of their American-born children.

After 1910, when U.S. laws required immigrants entering the country from the west to go through San Francisco, most Japanese immigrants settled in California. With their success in farming and the increased immigration of Japanese women, stable Japanese-American communities took shape in the 1920s.

Department of Commerce and Labor

Nineteen-year-old Tou Hasegawa (left) was a picture bride who came to the United States to meet her husband, Kunitaro (right), a California farmer, in September 1913.

Celebrating Tofu

Starting in 1996, Japanese Americans in Los Angeles have held a week-long festival each July honoring one of the most well-known Japanese foods: tofu.

Tofu is made from the "milk" of soybeans. This thick liquid is made by soaking soybeans in water until they swell to three or four times their normal size. The beans are then ground into a pasty liquid, which is then strained through a cloth: This strained liquid is the soybeans' "milk."

Next, the soy milk is heated and an ingredient called *nigari* is added. *Nigari* causes the milk to separate into solids and a watery liquid called whey. The solids are poured into molds, which form the block shapes of tofu that are sold in stores, and covered in cold water.

Tofu is healthful and easy to cook. At the tofu festival in Los Angeles, some of the most popular restaurants in the city set up booths to sell tofu dishes such as tofu tacos, tofu cheesecake, tofu ice cream, and tofu lasagna.

In towns and cities in agricultural regions, *nihonmachi*, "Japan Towns," began to appear. Small businesses, such as hotels, restaurants, and barbershops, were established. Some Japanese Americans opened general stores and drove regular routes to the local farms to deliver food and other supplies.

Meanwhile, the ability of Japanese Americans to succeed was constantly challenged by the nativist groups such as the IRL, which wanted to further reduce the number of immigrants allowed. The Immigration Act of 1924 granted the nativists their wish. This law ended almost all immigration to the United States. It was structured so that no Asian immigrants at all were allowed into the country. The Immigration Act of 1924 stopped Japanese immigration to the United States for nearly 30 years. Soon, another event would ensure that immigration from other areas would all but stop as well.

That event was the Great Depression. During this difficult economic period, which began in the fall of 1929, businesses and banks across the country failed. By 1932, one of every four American workers was jobless. During this period, the United States was not the land of opportunity it had always been.

An Impossible Situation

Like most Americans, Japanese Americans found that jobs were scarce during the Great Depression. But in many ways the Japanese Americans' situation was harder to deal with. For instance, if Japanese Americans tried to participate in American organizations such as labor unions or groups that offered help to the jobless, they were accused of interfering with white Americans' business. Yet when they remained among other Japanese in Japan Towns, they were seen as being too secretive and acting un-American. Japanese Americans were often not accepted as Americans, yet they had been in the United States too long to feel connected to Japan. Unfortunately, world events would soon make their situation even worse. 🎌

Opposite: *At the start of World War II, discrimination and hysteria surrounding Japanese Americans led to laws ordering families to be placed in internment camps. In this photo, taken in April 1942 in San Francisco, a little boy sits atop his family's belongings after they were forced to leave their home.*

Chapter Four

War and Internment

A New Level of Prejudice

Japanese Americans in the 1930s

The U.S. Census of 1930 listed about 280,000 people of Japanese descent living in the continental United States and Hawaii. Slightly more than half of that number lived in Hawaii. Nearly all of the approximately 138,000 Japanese Americans living on the U.S. mainland lived in California, Oregon, and Washington.

Over the first three decades of the 20th century, the efforts of anti-immigration groups to prevent Japanese immigration to the United States had been mostly successful. The immigration of Japanese men had been virtually ended by the 1907 Gentlemen's Agreement. All Japanese immigration had been ended by the Immigration Act of 1924.

Japanese Names

Certain syllables in Japanese surnames indicate places of origin or other information. *Naka*, for example, means "middle." *Mura* means "village." Thus, the surname Nakamura originated in a small town in central Japan. *Ta* means "rice paddy" (a field where rice is grown). Thus, the surname Tanaka originated in a region of rice farming in central Japan.

Traditional Japanese first names for girls almost always end in *ko*, which means "child." Common female names are Akiko ("autumn child"), Haruko ("spring child"), Keiko, Kiyoko, Michiko, and Yoshiko ("good child").

Boys' names often indicate the order of birth, using the suffix *ro* to indicate a son. For example, there is Ichiro ("first son"), Jiro ("second son"), Saburo ("third son"), and so on. Other common male names are Hiroshi, Kenji, and Yoshi.

Japanese Immigration to America

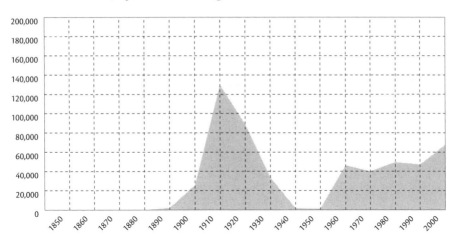

However, Japanese families continued to grow. As a result, more than 60 percent of all Japanese Americans in the 1930 census had been born in the United States. These nisei, or second-generation Japanese Americans, grew up with the shared cultural heritage of both Japan and America.

Like most immigrant children of the time, nisei worked with their parents to build lives based on traditional American values that focused on family, education, and religion. After attending local public schools, young nisei helped on family farms and in family-owned businesses. For their parents, the first-generation issei, however, preserving Japanese culture was also important. This culture was maintained by having the children attend Japanese language schools after regular school, by attending performances of Japanese plays and music, and by practicing the Buddhist or Shinto religion.

Despite efforts by the Japanese to be part of two worlds, the constant anti-Japanese prejudice in the United States caused a number of issei and nisei to leave the United States for Hawaii. There, Japanese immigrants had become a large segment of the population. More than 20,000 Japanese Americans moved to Hawaii from the United States during the 1930s.

Japanese forces entered Manchuria in China in 1931 with plans to domi-nate Asia. Relations with the United States began to suffer as a result.

Many of the Japanese who did stay in the United States turned to organizations such as the Japanese American Citizens League (JACL) to represent them in legal and political matters. Many other local Japanese-American groups also formed during the 1930s for the same reason. These groups usually gave them-selves names that included words such as *loyalty* or *citizens* to underline their American connection. This was one way to demonstrate that despite their heritage and the prejudice they faced, they still thought of themselves as Americans and felt loyal to their adopted homeland.

Japan's March to War

Throughout the 1930s, as the United States struggled through the Great Depression, Japan set off on a course that would lead it to war and, eventually, almost total destruction. In less than a century, Japan had gone from being a country behind the times to a modern industrial power.

When Emperor Hirohito took the throne in 1927, a powerful version of the traditional Shinto religion arose. This religion regarded the emperor as godlike and glorified the traditional Japanese virtues of obedience and self-sacrifice. Japanese leaders felt that Western nations such as the United States were greedy, individualistic, and racist. The feelings promoted under Hirohito are known as nationalism.

Those in control of Japan's government believed that their country should become a world-dominating empire. They spent enormous amounts of money to build up Japan's military. To spread their nationalism to the Japanese people, they filled the radio airwaves (there was no television at the time) with patriotic propaganda. These messages praised the superiority of the Japanese people and ridiculed other peoples and nations. This propaganda built public support for Japanese rulers as they began to carry out a plan to make Japan the most powerful nation in Asia. In 1931, Japanese forces invaded Manchuria in northern China and Shanghai in the south, establishing a foothold on the Asian mainland.

It's a Fact!

During Japan's 1937 attack on China, a U.S. Navy patrol boat stationed in Chinese waters, the *Panay*, was accidentally sunk, killing two Americans. Although Japan apologized for the act and paid to replace the boat, the incident caused severe strain between the United States and Japan.

In 1937, Japan launched an all-out attack on China. Over the next few years, relations between Japan and the United States grew tense as well. In late 1940, the United States prohibited the sale of military supplies to Japan and canceled a trade treaty between the two countries. These American actions led the Japanese army minister, Tojo Hideki, to call for a war of "self-defense and self-preservation."

The first battle of that war was Japan's surprise air attack at the U.S. naval base in Pearl Harbor, Hawaii, on December 7, 1941. Twenty-one ships were sunk or damaged and 323 aircraft were destroyed. In all, 2,388 people were killed and 1,178 were wounded. It was the greatest loss of life in an attack on the United States until the terrorist attacks of September 11, 2001.

Japan's surprise attack on Pearl Harbor on December 7, 1941, was a response to the U.S. decision to prohibit sales of weapons to Japan and withdraw from the trade treaty between the two countries. The attack prompted America's entry into World War II.

On December 8, 1941, the United States declared war on Japan and on Japan's allies, Nazi Germany and Italy. This marked the entry of the United States into World War II, the deadliest war in human history.

The Internment

L ike most Americans, Japanese Americans viewed the actions of Japan during the 1930s with great alarm. Few had strong connections to the country, especially to its new military leadership. The idea of the emperor as a godlike figure was as strange to them as it was to most other Americans.

The attack on Pearl Harbor enraged all Americans, including Japanese Americans. Japanese American Ron Oba was 17 at the time of the attack. "I was angry, very angry, that the Japanese would attack my country," Oba said. "I was an American." Besides being shocked and angry, Japanese Americans in the United States were also frightened. In a 2001 interview, a woman, Akiko K., recalled the events of December 7, 1941, when she was a young nisei in California. "I'd just come home from church. My father said, 'There's going to be trouble for us . . . Japan just bombed Pearl Harbor.' I thought, 'Why should [anyone] bother me? I'm an American.' [But] when I went to school that following morning, one of the teachers said, 'You people bombed Pearl Harbor.' All of a sudden I no longer felt equal . . . I felt nervous."

Not surprisingly, the attack on Pearl Harbor increased the fears and suspicion created by decades of anti-Japanese prejudice. Within days of the attack, curfews prohibited Japanese Americans living on the West Coast from being outside of their homes between 8 P.M. and 6 A.M. In addition, the Federal Bureau of Investigation (FBI) arrested more than 2,000 so-called enemy aliens. Among those arrested were Japanese-American community organization leaders, Buddhist and Shinto priests, newspaper editors, and language instructors. These people, many of whom were American citizens, were considered suspicious because of their positions in the Japanese-American community.

Few Americans in the early days of the war, however, were concerned about the rights of Japanese Americans. In fact, as tensions had risen between the United States and Japan during 1941, federal authorities had used Census Department information to develop a "watch list" of Japanese Americans. That year, Yoshiko Uchida, now a well-known children's-book writer, was a senior at the University of California at Berkeley, where her family lived. On December 7, she returned from studying to find her father gone. Her mother explained that FBI agents had taken him "for questioning" because it was known that he had been born in Japan. "My parents' loyalty to the United States was strong," Uchida wrote many years later. "He was arrested because he looked like the enemy."

Fear and hatred of Japanese Americans reached far above the level of Akiko K.'s schoolteacher or even of the FBI agents who took Uchida's father. A week after the attack on Pearl Harbor, Congressman John Rankin gave a speech in the House of Representatives in which he stated, "I'm for catching every Japanese in America . . . and Hawaii now and putting them in concentration camps. . . . Let's get rid of them now!"

In January 1942, the state of California ordered that all state employees of Japanese descent be fired from their jobs. By that time, strong support had arisen for a law to place all Japanese Americans in internment camps away from the West Coast. Doing so, supporters of the internment believed, would prevent Japanese Americans from helping Japanese forces if the Japanese invaded the U.S. mainland.

Secretary of War Henry Stimson supported the internment of Japanese Americans. In early 1942, Stimson told reporters, "their racial characteristics are such that we cannot understand or ever trust the . . . Japanese." His remark was one of many similar opinions expressed by government leaders.

As a result of this anti-Japanese sentiment, President Franklin Roosevelt signed Executive Order 9066 on February 19, 1942. This order authorized the military to remove any person from any area of the country where national security was threatened. Although the order did not mention any specific group or recommend detention, it was clear that Executive Order 9066 was aimed at Japanese Americans.

In 1942, the members of this Japanese family were sent from their home on Bainbridge Island, off the coast of Washington State, to an internment camp in California. Japanese Americans were removed from any region where national security was thought to be threatened.

Executive Order 9066 was the first step in a program that uprooted Americans of Japanese ancestry from their West Coast communities and placed them under armed guard for up to four years. More than 120,000 Japanese Americans, including almost 70,000 American citizens, were interned in camps far away from their homes.

Japanese Americans were shocked when Roosevelt signed the executive order. Most were deeply insulted by the suspicions of their fellow Americans. They thought of themselves as Americans first, and now they were considered enemies simply because of their race.

Some Japanese Americans took legal steps to protest these actions. One case involved Mitsuye Endo, who was fired from her state job in California and ordered to a detention center. Endo protested that her rights were being violated. She was an American citizen with a brother serving in the U.S. Army. A lawyer representing Endo filed a lawsuit in July 1942 against the U.S. government.

The Endo lawsuit was one of a series of court cases that would slowly make their way to the Supreme Court. As in most cases to be heard by the nation's highest court, however, the legal process would take years. Meanwhile, Japanese Americans tried to understand why their country had turned against them.

Mary Tsukamoto, a teenager in central California in 1942, recalled her shock at Roosevelt's actions. "We were busy raising strawberries, and harvesting crops that would really help our nation. We couldn't believe that they would need all of us to quit our work to produce our fruit, food for victory . . . and then be put away."

Meanwhile, there was no such anti-Japanese feeling in Hawaii even though the territory, the site of Pearl Harbor, was located 3,000 miles (4,800 km) closer to the enemy. More than a third of Hawaii's population was Japanese American. Yet Lieutenant

General Delos Emmons, the military commander in Hawaii, decided that "military necessity" there required the Japanese Americans to remain free and help in the war effort as soldiers and for support of the American forces stationed in the islands.

The first action of the U.S. military under Executive Order 9066 was to remove the entire Japanese-American community from Terminal Island off the shores of Los Angeles on February 25, 1942. Armed soldiers marched into the old fishing village and ordered every person of Japanese descent, including American citizens, to leave their homes within 48 hours. Soon Japan Towns in California, Oregon, and Washington were under the same orders.

The U.S. military's Western Defense Command quickly converted 16 locations in California—horse racetracks, fairgrounds, rodeo grounds, and labor camps—into temporary detention camps. The camps were surrounded by barbed-wire fences, which were patrolled by soldiers with bayonet-tipped rifles. Guard towers were manned by soldiers with machine guns, and searchlights crisscrossed the grounds at night. All of these measures were taken to be sure that no one would escape from the camps.

Barracks and horse stalls were divided into blocks with a central mess hall (cafeteria), latrine (bathroom), showers, washbasins, and laundry tubs. Toilets, showers, and bedrooms were open, with no privacy. There was no water or plumbing in the living quarters. Anyone using the latrine at night was followed by a searchlight.

Eight-person families were placed in 20-foot by 20-foot (6-m by 6-m) areas. Six-person families were placed in 12-foot by 20-foot (3.6-m by 6-m) rooms. Smaller families and single people shared open space with strangers. Each person received a straw mattress and an army blanket. Much of each day was spent waiting in line to eat, wash, or attend to personal needs. Poor sanitation and food quality led to frequent outbreaks of diarrhea and diseases such as tuberculosis and typhoid fever.

These Japanese Americans were interned at Camp Santa Anita in California and photographed in 1942.

Mary Tsukamoto recalled the events of early 1942 when her family was forced to report to Fresno, California:

> *[At] the Fresno Assembly Center . . . there was the barbed wire gate . . . we saw all these people behind the fence . . . hanging onto the wire, and looking out because they were anxious to know who was coming in. I will never forget the shocking feeling that . . . we were going to also lose our freedom. . . . And the [soldiers] with their guns and . . . bayonets. I don't know . . . if they thought we were going to run away. . . . When the gates were shut, we knew that we had lost something . . . very precious . . . we were no longer free.*

While Japanese Americans were held in these temporary detention camps, the War Department built 10 large internment camps, designed to hold about 12,000 prisoners each. Two of these camps, Manzanar and Tule Lake, were located in the California desert. Others were built in Arizona, Arkansas, Colorado, Idaho, Utah, and Wyoming.

Conditions at the camps were as bad as those at the temporary detention centers. After living for four months in a horse stall, Yoshiko Uchida and her sisters and mother were reunited with her father at the internment camp in Topaz, Utah, located in a dry, dusty lake bed. There they became family #13453. "With each step we sank two or three inches deep . . . dust crept into our eyes, mouths, noses, and lungs," Uchida recalled many years later. "Our energy went into keeping our room dusted, swept, and mopped."

The process of assembling and relocating Japanese Americans continued through 1942. Meanwhile, in June 1942, United States forces won a key naval battle at the Pacific Island of Midway, west of Hawaii. From that point on, the United States was never threatened by Japanese invasion. Yet the internment of Japanese Americans continued.

Japanese Americans confined to the internment camps attempted to live as normally as possible. Political associations, religious services, dances, and athletic competitions were part of the camp life. Although textbooks, paper, and other supplies were limited, schools were opened with teachers who volunteered to work in the camps.

Finally, on December 17, 1944, a congressional order, Public Proclamation Number 21, ended the mass internment of Japanese Americans. The following day, the U.S. Supreme Court ruled on the cases that had begun in 1942. The most important ruling came in the Mitsuye Endo case. The Supreme Court ruled that holding American citizens against their will when they had committed no crime was illegal. The justices ruled that Endo "should be given her liberty" and be returned to her job with the state of California, since her loyalty was clearly established. In the decision, the Court stated that "detention in Relocation

Centers of persons of Japanese ancestry . . . is an example of the unconstitutional [against the U.S. Constitution] resort to racism inherent in the entire evacuation program."

The congressional order and the Endo decision were the first steps in ending the internment of Japanese Americans. Because of the enormous task of returning the Japanese to their homes, however, the camps emptied slowly. Each individual received $25 and tickets for transportation home.

Beginning a life after the camps was difficult for many issei and nisei. In many cases, those who were interned had no homes, land, or businesses to return to. Many had been forced to sell their belongings at far below their value in the rush to evacuate. Others had lost lands they had leased and farmed. Many returning Japanese Americans discovered that their homes and businesses had been taken over by other Americans.

In the end, the internment of most Japanese Americans lasted from February 1942 until December 1944. Not all Japanese Americans who were interned remained in the camps for the entire period, however. In February 1943, the government began to administer loyalty tests to all internees over the age of 17. More than 35,000 internees who passed the tests were allowed to resettle in areas away from the West Coast.

Many Japanese Americans objected to the loyalty tests, and some internees refused to take them. Those who refused or who created other problems for authorities in various camps were segregated in the Tule Lake camp in California. The last 70 internees of the more than 120,000 Japanese Americans imprisoned by the U.S. government left Tule Lake on March 20, 1946, nearly seven months after the end of World War II. ❀

Opposite: *In May 1945, a Japanese family returned from an internment camp in Idaho to find their home in Seattle, Washington, vandalized with anti-Japanese graffiti and broken windows.*

Chapter Five

Advancement and Apology

"A National Mistake"

After the War

World War II ended in Europe in May 1945. In August 1945, the United States dropped atomic bombs on the Japanese cities of Hiroshima and Nagasaki. The war in the Pacific ended a short time later, and a devastated Japan was occupied by American forces. Japan's hopes of building an empire had been crushed.

The end of World War II marked the end of a painful period for Japanese Americans. It also marked the beginning of a change in their location and their lives. In 1941, almost all Japanese Americans lived on the West Coast. After the war and internment, most Japanese Americans had to completely rebuild their lives. More than 60,000 Japanese Americans decided to settle elsewhere in the United States.

The U.S. government, as well as church and volunteer groups, attempted to help Japanese Americans in the first years after the war. The government's G.I. Bill helped thousands of nisei who had fought in the war to attend college.

Nevertheless, in 1948, Japanese Americans were reminded that the prejudice they had encountered before the war still existed. That year the U.S. government investigated the internment. When the investigation was over, the Evacuation Claims Act was passed. Under this law, money was to be paid to Japanese Americans who had suffered economically during the internment. They would receive 10 cents for every dollar of property value that they could prove they had lost as a result of their internment. For example, if a Japanese-American family lost $1,000 worth of property, they would receive $100 under the Evacuation Claims Act. But even claiming this small amount of money was difficult. Japanese Americans had to provide documents proving they had lost their land, home, or other valuable belongings. Many such documents had been lost or destroyed. Not only were Japanese Americans cheated out of the full value of what they had lost, many were unable to prove they had lost anything at all.

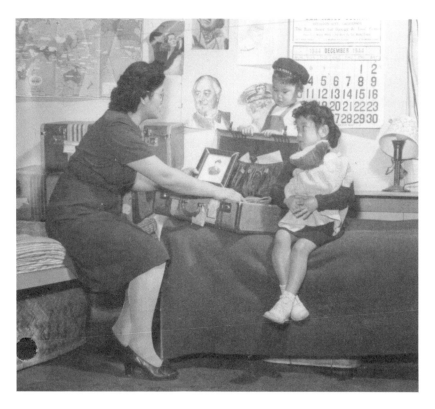

A Japanese family packs to travel home from an internment camp in 1945.

Breakthrough in Hawaii

While Japanese Americans on the U.S. mainland struggled to resume their lives after World War II, those in Hawaii were able to make great progress. People of Japanese descent were the largest segment of Hawaii's population, making up nearly 40 percent of the islands' population by the 1950s. Although their early years in Hawaii as contract laborers were marked by discrimination, Japanese Americans had achieved notable political power in the territory by the end of the 1940s.

Another boost for Japanese Americans in Hawaii came in 1952 from an unlikely source—the McCarren-Walter Act. Certain parts of this immigration law helped Japanese Americans. For example, it allowed all Asians living in the United States and its territories, including Hawaii, to become citizens. It also allowed 2,000 Asians to enter the country each year. The 1924 immigration act had outlawed Asian immigration entirely.

Under the McCarren-Walter Act, issei in Hawaii were able to become citizens and vote for the first time. In 1954, a group of young nisei politicians, led by Daniel Inouye, who had lost an arm in battle during World War II, were elected to Hawaii's legislature.

From 1954 until the end of the decade, Hawaii's leaders worked to make the islands a state. Their effort succeeded in 1959, when Hawaii became the 50th state. Japanese Americans were then elected to the U.S. Congress for the first time. In 1962, Spark Matsunaga was elected to the House of Representatives. That same year, Daniel Inouye was elected senator from Hawaii, a

Daniel Inouye, a World War II hero, was the first Japanese American to be elected to the U.S. Senate.

position he still holds more than 40 years later. Matsunaga and Inouye were the first Japanese Americans elected to Congress. In 1965, Patsy Takemoto Mink became the first Japanese-American woman to be elected to the House of Representatives.

On the Mainland

While Japanese Americans living in the United States were not able to achieve as much as Hawaiian Japanese in the early 1950s, they did gain some acceptance.

The McCarren-Walter Act, which helped Japanese immigrants in Hawaii, also helped Japanese Americans on the mainland. Issei were allowed to vote for the first time under the act. By the mid-1950s, Japanese Americans had been elected to local councils in cities with large Japanese-American populations, such as Los Angeles, San Francisco, and San Jose, California.

Also, although the 2,000 Asian immigrants allowed per year under the McCarren-Walter Act was not a large number, it resulted in the immigration of several thousand Japanese students, business executives, engineers, and other professional workers over the years.

War Brides

The largest group of Japanese immigrants during the 1950s, however, consisted of Japanese women who had married American soldiers after World War II. Known as war brides, they were allowed to enter the United States under the War Brides Act of 1945. This law allowed foreign-born wives of American citizens who had served in the U.S. armed forces to immigrate to the United States.

However, a law allowing Japanese women married to American servicemen to immigrate did not mean that they were welcomed in the Unites States. In fact, many war brides faced great difficulties adjusting to life in their new country. Unlike other Japanese immigrants, they usually did not settle in areas where other Japanese lived or where the Japanese language was spoken. Many of the war brides settled in the hometowns of their husbands and were the only Japanese in their communities.

The statistics on how many Japanese war brides immigrated to the United States vary widely, from several thousand to more than 25,000. This is because until 1967 it was illegal in many parts of the United States for people of different races to marry. Because these Japanese women were married to white, Hispanic, and African-American men, many of these marriages were not recorded, and many war brides lived in virtual seclusion.

On the Web site of the Japanese American Network (JA*Net), an organization based in Los Angeles, adult children of Japanese war brides and American servicemen communicate with one another. These Japanese Americans, who call themselves "JAs," provide examples of what life was like for Japanese war brides and their families:

"My mother [was] a 'war bride' and I was born in Tokyo a few months before we moved here. My interest in the whole JA experience derives originally from my mother's silence about her childhood/adolescence during the war in Tokyo: in the very few times when she spoke of it, she described the horrors of the fire-bombings in 1945. She tried to protect me from racism by saying as little as possible about her experience and her Japanese-ness, and so naturally I became curious."

Another child of a war bride responded: "My mother was a 'war bride' who became a single mother . . . with very little English . . . and no money. Somehow . . . she has discovered other Japanese immigrant women, but back when she became a poor single mother, most of her friends lived in our neighborhood. . . . And all of them were white."

Another writer adds: "My [mother] never taught me Japanese and never spoke it, even in private. Only my grandparents spoke to me in Japanese and I only saw them about two times in my life. I am really sorry to be such a terrible JA but my folks just hated Japan and anything Japanese after the war."

Taiko Drumming

One of most popular forms of music to come from Japan to the United States is *taiko* drumming. While drums have been used in Japan for centuries for military and religious purposes, the musical style of group drumming known as *taiko* has existed only since the 1950s.

In Japanese, the word *taiko* literally means "fat drum." Today the word *taiko* refers to the act of *taiko* drumming and to the drum itself.

Taiko was developed in Japan after World War II, when, in 1951, Japanese jazz drummer Oguchi Daihachi discovered some old music using *taiko* drums and assembled a group of drummers to perform it using drums of different sizes. He thus formed the first *taiko* group and a brand-new type of music was created. This blend of traditional instruments and modern rhythms became instantly popular in Japan.

Taiko came to the United States in the 1960s, when it was performed by Japanese Americans in California. Today, *taiko* is the one of the fastest-growing art forms in North America. In 1969 there were just two *taiko* groups in North America. Today there are more than 125 groups in more than 80 cities. *Taiko* festivals draw enthusiastic audiences and thousands of eager drummers. Performances by more than 1,000 *taiko* drummers at once, lasting for hours, are not unusual.

New Acceptance

The issei, the oldest generation of Japanese Americans, faced the greatest difficulties in the 1950s. Most had lost a great deal in the internment, including their homes and businesses, and were too old to start over. For many of these people, gardening became their main source of income. A survey taken in 1958, for example, found that almost three-fourths of issei-owned businesses in Los Angeles were gardening and yard-care operations.

Nisei, on the other hand, faced fewer obstacles. Most were well educated and spoke English. As hardworking as their parents, they quickly became successful in professional fields (jobs requiring higher education). A 1940 survey had found that only 4 percent of Japanese Americans were in professional fields. By 1960, more than 30 percent of Japanese Americans worked as professionals. By almost any measure, Japanese Americans had made great gains by the beginning of the 1960s.

Memory and Apology

As successful as Japanese Americans were in rebuilding and improving their lives after World War II, they still faced ignorance and prejudice. Popular culture of the time often depicted Japanese as stereotypes. Children's cartoons showed crude representations of Japanese in which they wore thick glasses and spoke broken English. Movies of the time also created unfair, damaging stereotypes. Throughout the 1950s, popular war films such as *Back to Bataan* and *The Bridge over the River Kwai* portrayed Japanese men as "glasses-wearing, cruel, [and] treacherous," wrote one film critic. Japanese women, in films such as *Sayonara,* were portrayed as meek, silly, or mysterious.

Japanese Monster Movies

During the 1950s, one type of movie created in Japanese film studios became extremely popular in the United States. These were the Japanese monster movies. The most famous of them was *Godzilla*, released in 1954. These movies were made during the first decade after the development of atomic weapons. Although the United States had dropped atomic bombs on Japan to end World War II, after the war the two nations became allies. The fear of nuclear war and the dangers of radioactive fallout were a deep concern for millions of people around the world.

The "monsters" of the Japanese films of the 1950s were all gigantic creatures that had been created by exposure to radioactivity. Godzilla was a 400-foot-tall (120-meter) reptile that resembled a dragon. Rodan was a monstrous bird of prey. Mothra was a giant flying insect.

Compared to today's sophisticated special effects, those in the Japanese monster films of the 1950s seem primitive. Yet these movies were enormously popular, especially with American children and teenagers. In a unique way, the movies helped build a connection between the two countries.

In the 1960s, important events in the United States brought change to the lives of Japanese Americans. One was an effort to increase immigration. The effort was led by President John F. Kennedy, who expressed his belief that if the United States considered itself a leader of the "free world," the anti-immigration law of 1924 was un-American. The law, Kennedy said, "had no basis in either logic or reason." After Kennedy's death in 1963, President Lyndon Johnson urged Congress to honor Kennedy in part by reforming immigration laws. Johnson's effort resulted in the passage of the Immigration Act of 1965. Under this law, Japanese immigration to the United States increased from less than 2,000 to about 4,500 people per year. Most of these immigrants settled in Hawaii.

The new law also said that immigrants could enter the United States if they could find jobs in professional fields where there was a shortage of qualified American workers. As a result, about 20,000 Japanese immigrants came to the United States over the next decade.

It's a Fact!

Most of the 20,000 Japanese immigrants who came to the United States during the late 1960s and early 1970s were college-educated professionals who worked in fields such as engineering, medicine, and scientific research.

The second event that brought change for Japanese Americans was the civil rights movement. This was the decade-long effort by African Americans to achieve equal rights after enduring centuries of slavery, racism, and brutality from white Americans. The determination and pride of African-American leaders such as Dr. Martin Luther King Jr. inspired many other minority groups to seek equal rights. One of these groups was the Japanese Americans, who felt that the internment had been overlooked as one of the key events in U.S. history.

During this time of great social change, many Japanese Americans started to question why the United States government had never accepted blame for the internment. To call attention to the issue, in December 1969 a group of about 150 mostly young Japanese Americans drove by car and bus to the eastern desert of California. There they staged a protest at the long-abandoned internment camp at Manzanar.

This event was reported in the news all over the country and became known as the Manzanar Pilgrimage. For many young Americans of all races, it was their first introduction to a little-known event that had occurred more than 25 years before. Soon, the movement to force the government to accept responsibility for the internment gained momentum. In 1970, the Japanese American Citizens League (JACL) called for the U.S. government to pay money to the people who had been interned. Congressman Norman Mineta of California, a Japanese American who had been interned at age 10 with his family, introduced this resolution in Congress in 1972.

Soon Japanese Americans began writing books about the experience of being interned. Some of these books were written for young people, and stories of the internment suddenly became an important subject in American literature. Yoshiko Uchida, for example, wrote *Journey to Topaz*, a fictional story based on her family's imprisonment in the camp at Topaz, Utah. In 1973, Jeanne Wakatsuki Houston and her husband, James Houston, wrote *Farewell to Manzanar*, a true account of the internment camps. This book, which became one of the most widely read young adult books of the 1970s, introduced an entire generation of young Americans to the events surrounding the internment.

These political and cultural efforts eventually led to a formal

Patsy Takemoto Mink

Patsy Takemoto Mink, a third-generation Japanese American born in Hawaii in 1927, was elected to the U.S. House of Representatives in 1965. Mink served 12 terms in Congress. She became nationally known for her fierce fight to pass the Women's Educational Equity Act, known as Title IX. When the act became law in 1977, it prohibited inequality between men's and women's educational programs. Under Title IX, girls and women were guaranteed the right to participate in school sports, and schools were required to provide equal funding for men's and women's athletic programs in the same sports.

When Mink died in 2002, Congress honored her by renaming Title IX the Patsy T. Mink Equal Opportunity in Education Act.

apology to Japanese Americans on behalf of the U.S. government. On February 19, 1976, President Gerald Ford issued Proclamation 4417. The date was the 34th anniversary of President Franklin Roosevelt's signing of Executive Order 9066. Ford's proclamation stated:

February 19th is the anniversary of a sad day in American history. It was on that date in 1942 . . . that Executive Order 9066 was issued, resulting in the uprooting of loyal Americans. Over one hundred thousand persons of Japanese ancestry were removed from their homes, detained in special camps, and eventually relocated. . . . We now know what we should have known then—not only was that evacuation wrong, but Japanese-Americans were and are loyal Americans. On the battlefield and at home, Japanese-Americans . . . have [made] sacrifices and . . . contributions . . . to the well-being and security of this, our common Nation.

In conclusion, Ford stated:

. . . I call upon the American people to affirm with me this American Promise—that we have learned from the tragedy of that long-ago experience forever to treasure liberty and justice for each individual American, and resolve that this kind of action shall never again be repeated.

This statement, which included the admission that the internment was "a national mistake," brought some satisfaction to Japanese Americans. For many others, however, it represented only a first step. 🔹

Opposite: *In 2001, the National Memorial to Patriotism was unveiled in Washington, D.C. It honors those Japanese Americans who lost their lives serving the United States in World War II and those who suffered in internment camps. Nina Akamu, a Japanese-American artist who created part of the memorial, is pictured.*

Chapter Six

Assimilation in a New Century

Japanese Americans Today

The 1980s

The 1980 census found slightly more than 600,000 Japanese Americans living in the United States, mainly in Hawaii and California. The term that Japanese Americans often use to describe their population is *nikkei*. This term includes the four generations of people of Japanese descent in the United States. Among the *nikkei* are the issei, the elderly immigrant generation from Japan. Most of the nisei, the first generation of Japanese Americans born in the United States, were children during the internment. The children of the nisei, the second generation born in the United States, are called the *sansei*. The children of the sansei, the third generation born in the United States, are called the *yonsei*.

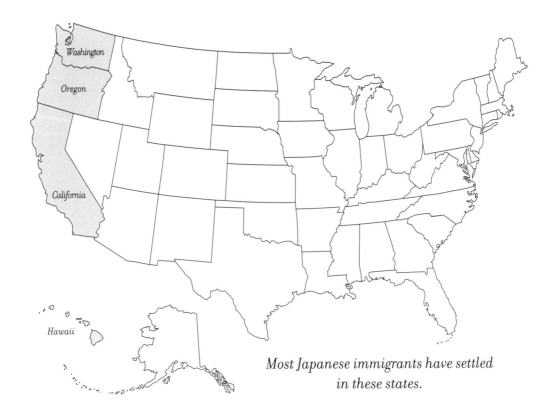

Most Japanese immigrants have settled in these states.

By 1980, the Japanese-American community, mostly sansei and *yonsei* by this time, had been largely assimilated into American society. The number of marriages between Japanese and non-Japanese had risen steadily for three decades. Surveys in San Francisco, Los Angeles, and Fresno, California, in 1990 revealed that almost 50 percent of Japanese Americans in those areas were married to non-Japanese.

Politically, Japanese Americans were well represented at local, state, and national levels. Japanese Americans used their political power to continue to press for justice for their elders who had suffered in the internment.

In 1980, Representative Mike Lowry of Washington, a state with a large Japanese-American population, introduced the World War II Japanese-American Human Rights Violations Act in Congress. This bill proposed payments of $15,000 per victim plus $15 for every day they were interned. Lowry's effort led to a congressional movement that made many Americans understand the lasting effects of the internment.

In 1981, Congress created the Commission on Wartime Relocation and Internment of Civilians (CWRIC). The purpose of the commission was to reexamine whether the forced removal and detention of Japanese Americans was as necessary to national security as many Americans had claimed at that time. The CWRIC held public hearings from July to December 1981 and heard testimony from over 750 witnesses. The emotional testimony of Japanese-American witnesses proved to be a turning point in the movement to address the internment. For many of the internees, it was the first time they had ever spoken about their wartime experiences.

In 1988, President Ronald Reagan (seated) signed H.R. 442 into law. Surrounding him are members of Congress who helped with the bill's creation and passage, including Senator Spark Matsunaga of Hawaii (far right).

In 1983, the CWRIC issued its recommendation that the U.S. government pay $20,000 to each of the 60,000 surviving internees. Even then, however, some Americans and members of Congress objected to the payment as well as to the government's admitting that it was wrong. It seemed that the powerful anti-Japanese racism that had been a driving force behind the internment in the first place had not completely died out. Because of this opposition, the recommendation of the CWRIC failed to pass in Congress.

After several years without taking action, the U.S. Senate entered the controversy over payments to Japanese-American internees. In 1987, Senator Spark Matsunaga of Hawaii introduced a bill that would give the surviving internees $20,000. The bill still faced opposition from some groups. By that time, however, the contributions of Japanese Americans to the United States were plainly visible.

Growing public support for the bill resulted in the Senate's passage of it in April 1988. The House followed with approval on July 4, 1988. The bill, named H.R. 442 after the 442nd Regimental Combat Team, the famed Japanese-American World War II fighting unit, was signed into law by President Ronald Reagan on August 10, 1988. It gave payments of $20,000 to each surviving internee and $1.25 billion for education for their descendants. In October 1990, the first nine payments were made at a ceremony in Washington, D.C. As the oldest surviving internee, Reverend Mamoru Eto of Los Angeles received the first check. Eto was 107 years old.

Into the Mainstream

Throughout the 1980s and 1990s, Japanese Americans continued to establish a presence in American culture. For example, in 1985, the world of classical music was amazed by the performance of Japanese-American violinist Midori Goto. Midori, who performs under her first name only, was born in Osaka, Japan. She showed musical ability early and began taking violin lessons at age three. At age 11, she was invited to study at the Juilliard School of Music in New York City and immigrated to the United States. Her professional debut as soloist with the Boston Symphony Orchestra in 1985 took place shortly after her 14th birthday. Midori has become one of the most admired classical musicians in the world.

In 1987, medical researcher Susumu Tonegawa was awarded the Nobel Prize in medicine for his groundbreaking research on the human immune system. Born in Japan in 1939, Tonegawa immigrated to the United States in 1963 to do cancer research. A college professor at the Massachusetts Institute of Technology in Boston, Tonegawa spent nearly 20 years researching the way the human body fights infection.

The Karate Kid

One of the most popular movies of 1984 was *The Karate Kid*. It tells the story of a white American teenager, Daniel, who moves to Southern California and strikes up a friendship with the Japanese gardener at his apartment complex, Mr. Miyagi. As the story unfolds, Daniel learns that Miyagi is a karate master and asks the older man to teach him.

When Daniel goes to Miyagi's home for lessons, he is awed by the tiny but beautifully landscaped gardens there, typical of homes in Japanese-American communities. Daniel becomes curious about Miyagi's background. He finds a box hidden in Miyagi's room. Inside are a Congressional Medal of Honor and a faded newspaper clipping about the death of a Japanese woman—Miyagi's wife—at the Manzanar camp.

Suddenly, Daniel, like millions of Americans who saw the movie, learns about a forgotten part of American history. In fact, the nisei soldiers of World War II won more medals than any other fighting unit. Many of them fought in the war while their loved ones were imprisoned. Many internees, especially women and children, died of diseases such as tuberculosis in the camps. Although *The Karate Kid* is remembered today for its emphasis on the martial arts, which had become very popular among Americans by the 1980s, its portrayal of Japanese-American life was one of the first in an American film.

The actor who played Mr. Miyagi, Noriyuki "Pat" Morita, had spent several years of his own childhood in an intern-ment camp. Morita became one of the most well-known Japanese-American television and movie actors of the last part of the 20th century.

Ann Curry

Growing up in Oregon, Ann Curry, like most children of the 1950s and 1960s, watched a great deal of television. Even as a child, she was interested in journalism. Watching the *Today* show at that time, however, she saw only white male reporters. "When you're a child and you don't see people like you doing something. . . . It's like looking through a shut glass door into a room that seems so tantalizing, but the door isn't open to you."

But by the 1990s, Curry's determination had paid off as she became one of television's most recognized faces. In contrast to earlier stereotypes of Japanese, in fact, Curry was named one of People magazine's "50 Most Beautiful People" in 1998.

In 1992, a Japanese-American athlete rose to worldwide fame during the Olympics at Albertville, France. Kristi Yamaguchi became a superstar in the United States when she won the gold medal in figure skating.

Japanese Americans also regularly appeared on television and in movies. Ann Curry, a newscaster on NBC's *Today* show since 1997, for example, first became nationally known as a reporter in the early 1990s. Japanese Americans also regularly appeared on television and in movies. Ann Curry, a newscaster on NBC's Today show since 1997, for example, first became nationally known as a reporter in the early 1990s. Tragically, another Japanese American was part of one of the most important news stories of the 1980s. Lieutenant Colonel Ellison Onizuka was among the seven astronauts killed in the explosion of the space shuttle Challenger on January 28, 1986. A native of Hawaii, Onizuka was a U.S. Air Force test pilot before training to become an astronaut.

At the end of the 20th century, Japanese Americans had become one of the most assimilated of all Asian immigrant groups. The century's end was also significant for Japanese Americans because on February 5, 1999, the U.S. Office of Redress Administration, the agency that distributed payments to internees, officially closed. By that time, the agency had verified and delivered $20,000 payments to 82,220 of the Japanese Americans who had been interned.

The closing of the Office of Redress Administration was followed by a related opening only two years later. In 2001, a symbol of the Japanese-American experience in World War II was unveiled to the public in Washington, D.C. Located just north of the U.S. Capitol was the newly constructed National Memorial to Patriotism. The memorial consists of a gentle stream of water flowing into a shallow pool. In the pool are five boulders, symbolizing the sometimes harsh relationship between Japanese Americans and the United States. In the center of the pool, two sculpted cranes (birds that are traditional symbols of good luck in Japan) fight to break free from barbed wire.

On the highly polished granite panels of the memorial are the names of more than 800 Japanese-American men who gave their lives in World War II. Also cut into the stone are the names of the camps where 120,000 men, women, and children, two-thirds of whom were native-born Americans, were imprisoned.

The memorial honors the courage and loyalty of Japanese Americans under terrible conditions during World War II. However, in the view of many Japanese Americans, the memorial also honors the U.S. government for the admission of its mistake and its formal apology. Those who were interned and have lived to see the changes in American society understand, perhaps more than most, the importance of living in a democracy.

"In the 1940s [Japanese Americans] had no power in Washington," said Morgan Yamanaka, an internee, during an interview in 2001:

Today, we have Senators, we have Congress people, we have mayors of cities. This would never happen [again] with the . . . Japanese . . . in the United States . . . but it might happen with another group, with no power. And therefore, I feel . . . [Japanese Americans] ha[ve] a responsibility to [remind others]. . . . I don't want it to happen to any other group of people.

Japanese Americans Serve Their Country

The terrorist attacks of September 11, 2001, caused the greatest loss of American life in a single day since the 1941 surprise attack on Pearl Harbor. The most well-known landmark destroyed in those attacks was the Twin Towers of the World Trade Center in New York City. Those huge buildings had been designed in 1965 by Japanese-American architect Minoru Yamasaki.

Yamasaki was born in 1912 in Seattle, Washington, to Japanese immigrant parents. He earned a degree in architecture from the University of Washington, where he paid his way by working in a salmon cannery. After moving to New York City in the 1930s, he worked with the architects who designed and built the Empire State Building. Yamasaki became famous for his designs of sleek international airport buildings, but his best-known design was the 1,360-foot-high (408-meter) towers of the World Trade Center.

On the day of the attacks, it became crucial to ground all airplanes in the United States in case other attacks were planned. Nationwide anti-terror procedures had to be established within hours. That task fell to the secretary of transportation, Norman Mineta. Mineta is a Japanese American who had been interned as a 10-year-old boy during World War II.

At the same time, the U.S. Army was on alert at home and around the world to prevent further attacks. The head of the U.S. Army on September 11 was General Eric Shinseki, a native of Hawaii who was the first Japanese American to command the U.S. Army.

The National Pastime

In 1910, a group of Japanese immigrants formed the San Jose Asahi baseball team in San Jose, California.

One of the strongest connections between Japan and the United States for more than 125 years has been baseball. The sport was introduced to Japan in 1872 by an American schoolteacher named Horace Wilson, who was teaching English to Japanese children. By the start of the 20th century, baseball had become Japan's most popular sport.

By the 1990s, the quality of the players in Japan caught the attention of major league baseball teams in the United States. In 1995, the first Japanese baseball player to enter the U.S. major leagues, pitcher Hideo Nomo, took the mound for the Los Angeles Dodgers.

Since that time, several Japanese have become successful major league baseball players. Outfielder Ichiro Suzuki of the Seattle Mariners is a fan favorite for his batting skills and lightning speed on the bases. In 2003, Japanese home run champion Hideki Matsui became a starting outfielder for the New York Yankees. New York newspapers referred to Matsui by his Japanese nickname, "Godzilla," after the famous 1950s Japanese movie monster.

Success and Ethnic Pride

In 2000, the U.S. Census counted the population of Japanese Americans at about 800,000 people. According to the census, the average Japanese-American family has three people. The average household income for Japanese Americans is more than $50,000, far above the national average for American families as a whole. Most Japanese Americans live in Hawaii and California. There are also large populations of Japanese Americans in Washington State, New York, and Illinois. The cities with the largest Japanese-American populations are Honolulu, Hawaii; Long Beach, California; New York City; San Francisco; Seattle, Washington; and Chicago, Illinois.

Japanese Americans had endured an uneasy relationship with their adopted homeland since the beginning of Japanese immigration. That, combined with the rapid economic growth that provided jobs and opportunities in Japan after World War II, made the Japanese the only Asian immigrant group to decline in numbers in the final decades of the 20th century. Japanese people chose to stay in their native country rather than immigrate to the United States. While the population of all Asian immigrants in the United States (almost 12 million people in 2000) showed an increase of more than 70 percent in the 10-year period between 1990 and 2000, the Japanese-American population recorded a decline of about 6 percent.

Most Japanese who immigrated to the United States in the final decades of the 20th century and who continue to immigrate today fall into two categories. Some are students, known as *ryugakusi,* who come to the United States for an education. These immigrants, who are high school or university students, may stay in the United States for five years. The other main group of Japanese who come to the United States is known as *shosha-nin.* These are Japanese businessmen who stay in the United States for a limited time. Some bring their families with them and some choose to stay in the United States permanently. Most, however, return to Japan.

While the number of immigrants from Japan declined, Japan's influence on American culture grew as the United States

Speaking Japanese

Here are a number of words commonly used in English that originated in Japanese or are taken directly from that language:

futon: a cotton-filled mattress used as a bed or a low couch

hibachi: a cooking device for grilling meat and vegetables

honcho: a person who takes charge of a situation or group

karaoke: a musical device that allows a person to sing along with a recorded song

ninja: a Japanese warrior from the time of the samurai, similar to a knight

tofu: a soft food made from soybean milk that often replaces meat in cooking

and Japan became partners in business. From the late 1960s on, for example, Japanese automobiles arrived in the United States in growing numbers. In 2003, one of every four cars sold in the United States was a Japanese car, such as a Toyota, Honda, or Nissan. Furthermore, Japanese car companies opened factories in the United States. In 2002, 70 percent of the Japanese vehicles bought by Americans were made in the United States.

Japanese technology has also had a powerful effect on everyday life in the United States. Televisions, appliances, music systems, and other products made in Japan have been sold in tremendous quantities in the United States for more than four decades. Brands such as Sony, Toshiba, and Yamaha are familiar names to millions of American consumers.

As they did in the 1950s with Japanese monster movies, American children of all ethnic backgrounds enjoy parts of Japanese culture that are aimed at them. In the 1980s, toys such as the "Transformers," plastic robots that could be changed into spaceships with a few easy movements, became enormously popular. Cartoon characters such as Pokemon, also developed in Japan, drew the attention of millions of American children.

Japanese foods also became part of the American diet. Dishes made from raw fish, seaweed, and rice, known as sushi, are sold in supermarkets and restaurants across the United States. Japanese food products such as tofu, made from soybeans, have become an important part of the diet of vegetarians and others who wish to eat healthy, low-fat foods.

The acceptance of Japanese culture in America has in many ways sped the assimilation of Japanese Americans into American society. The racist rejection of Japanese immigrants in the early 20th century and the bitterness toward Japan after World War II have declined as the two nations have shared economic and cultural ties.

As the 21st century began, the story of Japanese Americans has become one more chapter in the long history of immigration to the United States. Few groups among the many who have come to the United States have overcome more obstacles, and few have achieved greater success.

Time Line of Japanese Immigration

660 B.C.   First Japanese emperor takes the throne.

A.D. 1600   Tokugawa era begins and all Westerners are excluded from Japan.

1853   Commodore Matthew Perry leads a fleet of American warships into Edo (now Tokyo) Harbor, opening Japan for trade.

1868   Meiji era begins in Japan.

1869   First group of Japanese immigrants arrives in the United States.

1870   U.S. Census lists 55 Japanese immigrants in the United States.

1885   First Japanese laborers arrive in Hawaii to work in sugarcane fields.

1900   Hawaii becomes a U.S. territory.

1905   In May, the Asiatic Exclusion League (AEL) is formed in San Francisco. It is the first organized effort of the anti-Japanese movement.

1907   Japan and the United States agree under the Gentlemen's Agreement to halt the immigration of Japanese laborers to the United States. Japanese women are allowed to immigrate if they are wives of U.S. residents.

1913   California passes the Alien Land Law, forbidding "all aliens ineligible to citizenship" from owning land.

1922   In November, the U.S. Supreme Court reaffirms the ban on Japanese immigrants becoming U.S. citizens.

1924   Congress passes the Immigration Act of 1924.

1941   On December 7, Japan bombs U.S. ships and planes at the Pearl Harbor military base in Hawaii. Within 48 hours, the FBI arrests more than 2,000 Japanese-American community leaders.

1942   On February 19, President Franklin Roosevelt signs Executive Order 9066, requiring people of Japanese ancestry living in the western part of the United States to be transported to internment camps.

1943   In January, the War Department announces the formation of a segregated unit of Japanese-American soldiers and calls for volunteers.

1944   The U.S. Supreme Court rules in the Endo case that the Japanese intern-
        ment camps are unconstitutional.

1945   On August 6, the United States drops an atomic bomb on Hiroshima
        in Japan. On August 9, a second bomb is dropped on Nagasaki. Japan
        surrenders on August 14, ending World War II.

1946   The Tule Lake internment camp closes on March 20. It is the last camp
        to close.

1948   The Japanese American Evacuation Claims Act is passed. Its purpose is
        to repay Japanese Americans for losses during their internment.

1952   In June, the McCarren-Walter Act is signed into law, allowing Japanese
        immigrants to become U.S. citizens.

1962   Daniel Inouye of Hawaii becomes the first
        Japanese American elected to the U.S. Senate.

1965   Patsy Takemoto Mink of Hawaii becomes the
        first Japanese-American woman elected to the
        U.S. House of Representatives.

1976   President Gerald Ford signs a congressional
        proclamation calling the internment of Japanese
        Americans "a national mistake."

1981   Congress establishes the Commission on
        Wartime Relocation and Internment of
        Civilians (CWRIC).

1988   In August, President Ronald Reagan signs
        H.R. 442, which acknowledges the unjust
        internment of more than 110,000 people of
        Japanese descent and offers payment of
        $20,000 to each internee.

1990   On October 9, the first nine payments are
        made to surviving internees.

1995   Pitcher Hideo Nomo of the Los Angeles
        Dodgers becomes the first Japanese baseball
        player to compete in the major leagues.

1999   General Eric Shinseki becomes the first Japanese American to be named
        to the U.S. Army's top command position, chief of staff.

2001   In June, the National Japanese American Memorial opens in
        Washington, D.C.

        In October, Seattle Mariners outfielder Ichiro Suzuki becomes the first
        Japanese baseball player to win the Most Valuable Player (MVP) Award.

2004   Japanese-American congressman Michael Honda of California introduces
        a resolution recognizing February 19, the date in 1942 when President
        Roosevelt signed Executive Order 9066, as a National Day of
        Remembrance. The resolution passes unanimously.

Glossary

assimilate To absorb or blend into the way of life of a society.

contract laborer Worker who agrees to work for a specified length of time in return for living quarters, food, and a small salary.

culture The language, arts, traditions, and beliefs of a society.

democracy Government by the majority rule of the people.

emigrate To leave one's homeland to live in another country.

empire Political unit covering an extremely large area.

ethnic Having certain racial, national, tribal, religious, or cultural origins.

immigrate To come to a foreign country to live.

internment Imprisonment, especially during a time of war.

issei Japanese immigrants born outside of the United States.

nativism A prejudice in favor of people born in a nation and against immigrants who settle in that nation.

nihonmachi Japanese term for "Japan Towns," or communities of people of Japanese descent.

nikkei Japanese term for Japanese Americans.

nisei Second-generation Japanese Americans.

prejudice Negative opinion formed without just cause.

racism Belief that one race is better than others.

refugee Someone who flees a place for safety reasons, especially to another country.

stereotype Simplified and sometimes insulting opinion or image of a person or group.

Further Reading

BOOKS

Cooper, Michael L. *Fighting for Honor: Japanese Americans and World War II.* Boston: Houghton Mifflin, 2000.

Houston, Jeanne Wakatsuki, and James D. Houston. *Farewell to Manzanar.* Boston: Houghton Mifflin, 1993. Reprint, 2002.

Levine, Ellen. *A Fence Away from Freedom: Japanese Americans and World War II.* New York: Putnam, 1995.

Mattern, Joanne. *Japanese Americans.* Immigrants in America Series. New York: Chelsea House, 2003.

Perl, Lila. *Barbed Wire and Guard Towers: The Internment of Japanese Americans during World War II.* Tarrytown, N.Y.: Benchmark, 2002.

WEB SITES

Asian-Nation: The Landscape of Asian America. "442nd: Rescue of the Lost Battalion." URL: http://www.asian-nation.org/442.shtml. Downloaded on July 8, 2004.

Japanese American National Museum. URL: http://www.janm.org/main.htm. Downloaded on July 8, 2004.

J-net Central: Your Complete Source to Japanese, Japanese American, and Asian American Links. URL: http://www.nichibeitimes.com/links.html#jahist. Downloaded on July 8, 2004.

The Smithsonian National Museum of American History. "A More Perfect Union: Japanese Americans & the U.S. Constitution." URL: http://americanhistory.si.edu/perfectunion/experience/. Downloaded on July 8, 2004.

Index